AF592811

Way To Success

Dr. Rajesh Takyar

NU VOICE
PRESS

First published by NU VOICE PRESS 2025
An imprint of Hubhawks Pvt. Ltd
www.nuvoicepress.com

Copyright © Dr. Rajesh Takyar 2025

The moral rights of the author have been asserted
Database right Nu Voice Press (maker)

The characters and events portrayed in this book are fictitious. Any similarity to real persons, living or dead, is coincidental and not intended by the author.

No part of this book may be reproduced, or stored in a retrieval system, or transmitted in any form or by any means, electronic, mechanical, photocopying, recording, or otherwise, without express written permission of the publisher.

All rights reserved. Enquiries concerning reproduction outside the scope of the above should be sent to Nu Voice Press at the address above.

ISBN: 978-81-992047-7-5

Printed at Tomson Press (India Ltd)

Published by: Nu Voice Press

Disclaimer

The information in this book is provided for general informational purposes only. The author and publisher make no guarantees regarding the accuracy, completeness, or applicability of the content. Any reliance on this information is at the reader's own risk. This book does not constitute legal, medical, financial, or professional advice. Readers should seek professional guidance tailored to their specific circumstances.

The book may reference real individuals, events, or companies. Any such references are based on publicly available information and are included for educational and illustrative purposes. The author has made every effort to present these accounts accurately, fairly, and without malice. No intent exists to defame, misrepresent, or harm the reputation of any person, living or deceased. If any errors or misinterpretations are found, they are unintentional, and the author and publisher assume no responsibility for any consequences arising from them.

The author and publisher assume no liability for any loss, damage, or disruption caused by the use of this book. In no event shall they be responsible for any direct, indirect, incidental, consequential, or punitive damages resulting from its use.

This is a loving gift for the youth, geared to embark on a voyage that's rather long.

Preface

Every single being wants to be successful and keeps searching for ways and means to achieve this, and has to struggle in life. There are plenty of obstacles in this self-examination of a person. Which is the right way of enhancing life? It is very difficult to find one. We see many successful people around us, but how they accomplished it is quite complex to comprehend.

I have written this book with the very purpose of simplifying this difficult task. Once you read it, you will be amazed to know that what you were struggling to find outside and in others, is right there within you. You may have sought it from others, but no one could give it to you. With a little effort, you can bring it out from within yourself and become successful!

'You are successful' is not just a sentence. without a doubt, it will be a statement of fact of what you have achieved once you read this book.

If you are reading this book in the hustle and bustle of this fast-paced life with the inspiration to achieve the goal of your life, no one can stop you from reaching the heights of fulfillment in your life. My best wishes as well as my faith are with you.

Contents

CHAPTER 1:

The Importance of Understanding the Power of the Subconscious

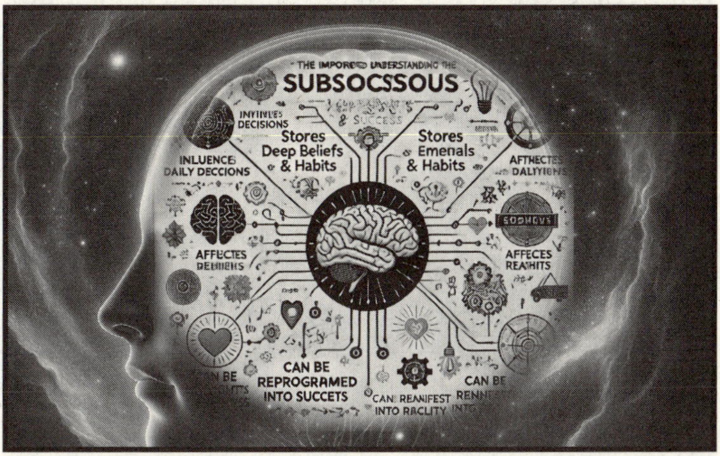

A person is born and grows up in due time. A lot is always happening around him; he notices it, but he is not able to do all of that. Only a select few are indifferent to what others do. But those with a strong consciousness have the desire to do a lot in a short time. They are highly concerned about what they experience right from childhood. They ponder about what a particular person possesses that I do not;

can I not become like him, etc.? This is where their struggles start. That's the time to get familiar with the subconscious mind. Our subconscious mind speaks to us if we listen. This clearly means that the powers of our subconscious mind can be awakened. If there is no such voice within someone's mind, it will take longer to activate it. Even with a little effort, the subconscious power in the human body starts saying that you too can become like that, and a person sets out on the quest for it.

You will think that I am a fool if I tell you that you are more powerful than your creator, god, or whatever other name you may be calling him. But it is the truth. Think about how you can transform the body and existence that he created. How can you do it if you are not bigger or more powerful? One may be born in a very poor family with insufficient means of livelihood, one could be differently abled due to one's actions, one can become rich or poor, a criminal, or one can even become a great saint or a *yogi*. Aren't you then bigger or more powerful than him?

People unaffected by such thoughts get stranded behind in the race of life. All their lives, they blame the creator who created them, and one day leave the world forever. They condemn their parents or god for everything.

When you watchfully try to understand your thoughts and habits, you get a glimpse of the subconscious mind. Ask yourself some questions like – what scares me, what do I often think about, which direction are my habits taking me in? The subconscious mind deduces simple and frequently repeated thoughts to be the truth. One should always think of success, happiness, and goals as if they are a reality in the present. When you react without thinking much, it is your subconscious mind's doing. Try to identify these habits and change these gradually in a constructive direction. Identifying the subconscious mind and connecting with it is a process. It won't happen at once, but it is definitely possible with continuous practice. One should have faith in one's ability and keep patiently proceeding towards the goal.

Identifying the subconscious mind is a journey in profundity. It is the sum total of a person's habits, beliefs and thoughts. It can be termed the active computer of the body. Those who work with computers know that when we do something with our mobiles or computers, a lot of the work is taking place on a cloud computer in the background and not on the mobile or computer that we are using. Steve Jobs used the term 'cloud' for it for the first time. The subconscious mind is the cloud computer of our body. If you learn to connect with it, a solution to each of life's problems will be possible and goals will be achieved.

Control your subconscious mind; it will bring discipline to your life.

***

Chapter 2:

Why Are Some People Successful While Others Are Not?

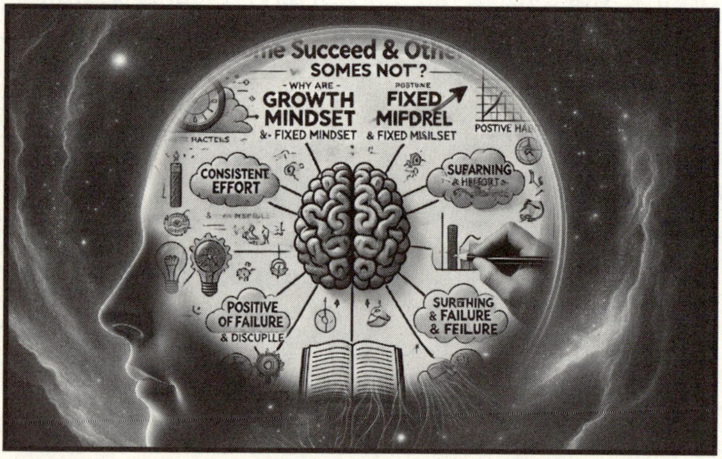

What is the distinction between successful people and failures? Does it arise from the *karma* of their past lives? Science does not accept it. There are some who completely deny it. I can offer an example in their favor. I came across this news only two days ago. It was about Harshvardhan from the Hassan district in Karnataka. He had worked very hard; his parents had supported him wholeheartedly and ensured that he got a good education. But destiny had something else planned! The day he was to join as an officer of the Indian Police Services (IPS), he met with an accident as the tire of the police vehicle burst, and he died on the road near Kittane in Hassan *Taluka*. He belonged to Madhya Pradesh and was a 2023 batch IPS officer of the Karnataka cadre.

Why did he reach the end before his journey had even started in the real sense? What is the truth behind such an incident taking place?

Hindu scriptures have a very good answer to this question. The hitch is, the sun of the knowledge of these scriptures is yet to rise at the dawn of life. Implying that till then, there is no time to study these. Scriptures state that we always carry the account of our past deeds with us. Why this happened with Harshvardhan can be a matter of reflection. But this is an exception.

In reality, whether a person succeeds or fails depends mainly on their thinking, determination, discipline, and subconscious mind. It is absolutely true that successful people look for solutions to problems while unsuccessful people focus on them.

If you think positively, have faith in yourself, work hard, and move forward with discipline, success is bound to follow. The path may be difficult, but if you keep moving, you will definitely reach your destination. Successful people learn from their mistakes and analyze themselves from time to time. Whenever they commit a mistake, they mull over where they went wrong and how it could have been improved. They learn from such letdowns and look at them as new beginnings. They consider it a learning experience and try to improve.

Unsuccessful people only blame others for their failures. If they try to analyze themselves, they are bound to realize their mistakes. But they consider failure to be the end and feel disappointed. They say, "I always fail. It is useless to try anymore." They have no goal or plan. They work haphazardly.

***

Chapter 3:

The Secret of Enduring Success

Some people are just different. They are successful, but are unable to handle it. That's because they have greater belief in their own actions than in time. After all, they have freshly tasted success. Success at such times is limited to material things, and mental, emotional, and spiritual balance is inconsequential. Their success does not spring from the depths of their souls. They start to feel that they will conquer the world. What they don't know is that everyone's life is defined by their *karma*. Bad *karma* brings bad times. One's success is of no use then.

Sachin Tendulkar and Vinod Kambli are examples of how this works. Initially, both contributed to Indian cricket at almost the same time. The same Guru groomed them both. They had been thick friends since childhood. Both established themselves as distinguished Indian cricket players and made a good name with their talent. They have many record partnerships to their name. But one look today, and we find that Sachin Tendulkar has had a career spanning 24 years from 1989 to 2013; he played 664 matches, making many national and international records. When he bid adieu to cricket, he was considered the 'God of Cricket.' He has been felicitated with awards like the 'Bharat Ratna'. Vinod Kambli, on the other hand, despite being a promising batsman, can't be considered successful. His career as a cricketer of just 9 years from 1991 to 2000, was very short. He played only 104 matches. Compared to Sachin Tendulkar, he leads an obscure and helpless life today. Sachin, on the other hand, is still an inspiration for the youth.

There has been only one difference. Sachin has been the very embodiment of hard work, discipline, and humility throughout his period of success. Vinod's personality, on the other hand, was marked by shades of aggressiveness and a lack of discipline. Success without purpose ultimately leads to a hollow victory.

Sachin had recognized the power of his subconscious mind at a young age. He remained completely involved singularly in cricket for a long time. He had realized that one cannot ride the horse of success for one's entire life. The sprint is bound to end someday. Racing ahead should not mean losing sight of the ground and not at all being mindful of what's happening around simply because you are flying high.

Just like Sachin, Vinod Kambli mounted the horse of success. However, halfway through, he got lost in the glamor and razzmatazz of films and reality shows. He found it more attractive. During that phase, Sachin remained completely devoted to cricket owing to the self-knowledge in his heart and the power of his subconscious mind. He started living every moment trying to improve. Vinod, on the other hand, did not heed the call of his subconscious, and the seriousness of his involvement in cricket was not enough. Difficulties started crossing his path with time. He had to face controversies many times. As compared to Sachin, Vinod Kambli does not seem to lack talent in any way. But his lack of discipline and stability was starkly visible. He might have achieved external success, but his life lacked relationships, marked by mental stress and loneliness. This made him unsuccessful from within.

Vinod too possessed the secret powers of the subconscious mind that Sachin or any successful person has. But he just kept racing, disregarding its call.

Mahatma Gandhi said, *"The measure of success is not wealth or power, but how peaceful and content you feel."*

***

Chapter 4:

Anything is Possible

Our subconscious mind is a storehouse of powers. Anyone can access those powers through it. But it has to be awakened to do so. No one can climb the pinnacle of success without ignoring it. If one does, it cannot last. The subconscious mind is an invisible and powerful aspect of our consciousness. It stores our childhood experiences, fears, habits, and positive or negative thoughts. It unconsciously influences most decisions in our lives. The subconscious mind has real control over our behavior and habits. It plays an important role in adopting new ideas and changing old habits from time to time.

We can envisage it to be like a closed box. If you store thorns in it and then forget about it, whenever you put your hand in that box, you are bound to get hurt. But if you keep a piece of velvet or silk in it, you will experience pleasure and softness when you put your hand in it. Negative thoughts in life are like thorns. They should never be stored.

To understand this, you have to erase the word impossible from your mind like Adolf Hitler did. You have to accept his words, "Those who believe in the impossible have accepted failure."

This is the first rule for believing in the powers of the subconscious mind. For a person whose subconscious powers are awakened, the word impossible is nonexistent. The word is a mental barrier that limits our thinking. You may not believe it if I tell you that it is through these powers that I have found God, but that is the truth. I have only read the word impossible; I don't comprehend its meaning. I could never understand the word impossible. I am also sure that after you have read half of this book, you will continue reading with faith in what I have said. Don't read this book just to complete it. You have to learn from it.

I once went to a place in Manali, agonized by the hustle and bustle of life and numerous troubles. Someone had told me that a holy man who lived near the Manikarn Valley helped people realize the powers hidden within them. I decided to meet that sage.

I set out in search of the sage's hut in the forests of Manali. The weather was frosty due to snow, and there was a dense silence in the forest. The day started to fade into twilight as I walked, and a feeling of nervousness started to grip my mind. All around me, there were just deodar trees and complete silence.

Suddenly, my sight fell on an ashram. I could see an old, saintly man from a distance. He sat on a rock in a meditative posture. His white hair and calm face exuded a divine feeling. The crimson glow of the sun setting in front of him made his face glow with a unique aura. Sunrays fell on his face, filtering through the branches of trees.

Tired, I went ahead and sat close to him. I was tired. A younger mystic also sat meditating close to him. I bowed to him and asked, "O sage, caught up in the struggles of life, I feel lost. Who am I? Is there any purpose in my life?"

He opened his eyes, "It's a big question, but its answer lies within you," he continued with a smile on his face, "First, look at this forest—it's calm, steady, and powerful. There is only balance here, no conflict."

Puzzled, I asked, "How does this answer my question, O' wise one?"

"Just like this jungle, power and peace are hidden inside your mind, but instead of searching for it, you get yourself entangled running all around. Your subconscious mind is your biggest power. Awaken it," he replied.

After answering a few more questions, the sage gave me a small practice: "Feel your breath, let it flow like the Beas River. Notice how life flows within you with every breath. Try to calm down your thoughts. Let them be steady like these trees. Any fear or doubt will come and fly away like a butterfly. Don't try to catch it. Repeat the sentence, "I am calm. I am powerful. My life has a purpose."

I followed his advice. The turmoil within me started to ebb down slowly. I began to feel as if a new light had dawned within me.

I then realized that all the answers are within and not outside us. One only needs to be silent to receive them.

***

Chapter 5:

Discovery of the Power of the Subconscious

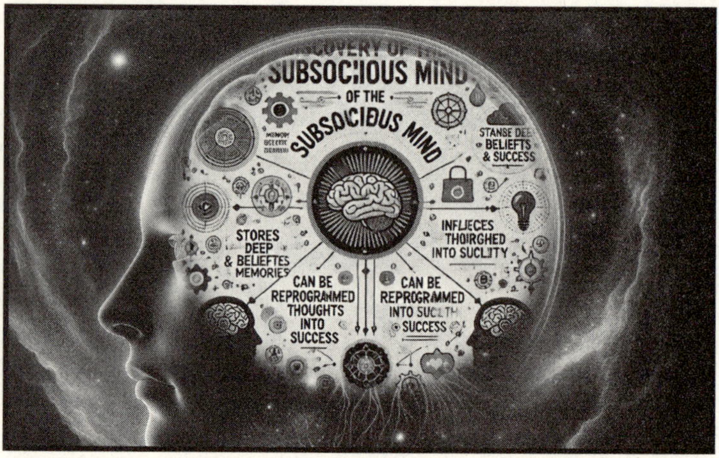

Andrew Carnegie, a successful American industrialist born in 1835, made huge efforts towards this. In his opinion, the time devoted to education all over the world was not adequate. What actually needed to be learnt wasn't taught. That is why he made a lot of effort to give its crux to the world. We will now discuss the same.

Thomas Edison, the great inventor born 12 years after him, probably understood this very early in life.

That is why he became such a great inventor with merely three months of schooling. People would find it difficult to believe that a person having more than 1000 patented inventions under his belt had received such a meager education. How could he accomplish this? It was because he had his own powers, he brimmed with self-confidence. His mother was also knowledgeable. His subconscious mind was full of powers.

American businessman, inventor, and visionary Steven Paul, 'Steve' Jobs, was famous as the co-founder, chairman, and Chief Executive Officer (CEO) of Apple Inc. A lot of credit for his success also goes to Indian wisdom. He did not achieve success immediately after establishing Apple in 1976. He also came to India in 1974 to learn the secret of awakening the latent energy of his mind. During his stay here, he developed a deep understanding of meditation, yoga, and Indian philosophy. It is here that he became aware of the immense source of power housed within every being, also known as the subconscious mind by the people here. It is only a matter of awakening it. A person who understands it is bound to bid adieu to this world as a successful man. He established Apple two years after learning this.

Death is an absolute truth. Steve Jobs was a successful man and a winner in life, but he could not conquer death, nor could he keep it far from his life. He is considered to be the greatest visionary and innovator of the modern era. He breathed his last on 5 October 2011 in Palo Alto, California. But he left behind a huge source of inspiration, touching the lives of many young people even after his death.

***

Chapter 6:

Why Does One Have to Have Everything?

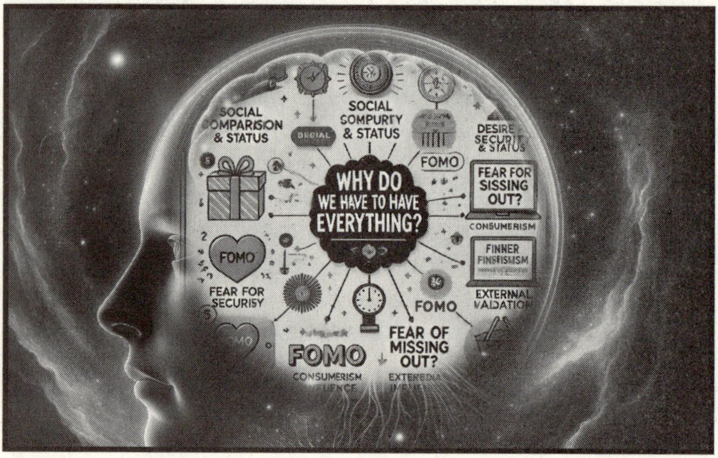

What's life after all if it's not a happy life, full of abundance of wealth and wanting in troubles and tribulations. This is how it has been right from the dawn of human life and holds true even today. There may be multiple simple ways of making this possible, which can be discovered. With this very idea in mind, Andrew Carnegie tried to create an account of the experiences of successful people of the world and made it available to people all over the world. It was nothing but the essence of the answers given by successful people to some questions. One thing that stood out from all those answers was that the powers of the subconscious minds of all those were fully awakened. Numerous people benefited from his effort and achieved success.

Do you feel that what you possess is the only thing? What others have is nothing? You may say that, actually, they are also things. Then why don't you have all of those? That is because no one can ever have everything. This implies that nothing is scarce. You cannot get everything, but you can certainly get plenty. Therefore, with a narrow mindset, one should not focus on what one lacks. All you need to do is learn how to acquire it. Hidden in the pages of this book, you will find a way to do so.

It is altogether a different matter that after attaining the heights of success in life, many successful people start wondering as to whom they did everything that they did. Was it for the family? The answer that comes from within is no. That's because by that time, they have acquired real knowledge. What happens then is that they keep little for themselves and distribute the rest among others. This is an ancient tradition that still continues. Andrew Carnegie thought similarly, too. He donated 350 million dollars (equivalent to billions of dollars today), about 90% of his total wealth.

"A man who dies rich dies disgraced," was Andrew Carnegie's opinion.

Every successful person ultimately wishes to write their autobiography. The aim is not to get more money or to get fame. The desire is to make others' paths easier by sharing one's own story. They possess a treasure trove of knowledge gained while solving their problems. They want to share and teach it to everyone.

Why is it that a person starts his life with struggle, seeks so much, and gives up everything in the end? This is not a philosophical question. The only answer to this is that after all the experiences of their life, their subconscious mind reveals to them the truth that in the end, everything is left behind. How the subconscious mind comes to such a conclusion is quite simple. The subconscious mind lives purely in the present; there is no past or future for it. This has later been explained in greater detail.

***

Chapter 7:

Where to Find This Power?

One does not get the powers of the subconscious mind from anywhere outside. They are very much within you. You have to understand this very clearly. Hindu *Puranas* and religious texts of other religions extensively discuss this. They clearly explain the secret of attaining it. Yoga, devotion, and meditation are easy ways prescribed to get them. But humans are in a constant state of dilemma. We seek instant gratification. We don't have time. If you look back and observe, you will find that those who have attained it have been patient enough to count waves sitting on the shore. Those who entered the ocean in a hurry to get out of it quickly were drowned.

Even a fisherman who goes into the deep sea in his boat finds fish only with a calm mind amid the ocean. He anchors at one spot and sits patiently, counting waves.

The path of yoga, devotion, and meditation to awaken the invisible power of the mind may seem slow, but it actually is not so. For it, one has to invest time in the beginning. But the results also start to show very soon. You need to just start your effort. This path impacts our thoughts, feelings, and the decisions in our lives. The problem of where to find the powers that bring us out of the difficulties of life and direct us towards success and peace is there for sure. The answer to it lies within you.

Understanding and using the power of the subconscious mind can make life positive and purposeful. We have two brains. We are aware of one, and we can get to know the other. The first part—the one we are cognizant of is that part of our brain which actively stores our experiences, thoughts, and habits. The other mind that we are unaware of stores our deepest habits, memories, emotions, and inner motivation. Surprisingly, it controls 90-95% of our mental activities. Therefore, knowingly or unknowingly, it plays a vital role in everyone's life. It is sure to play its role even if we fail to understand it, but in that case, it won't be agreeable to us. One may end up becoming Kambli rather than Sachin.

Swami Vivekananda once said, "Arise, awake, and stop not till the goal is reached." His greatest strength was his self-confidence. The power of self-confidence is the power of our subconscious mind.

***

Chapter 8:

Identifying the Powers

Have you ever truly loved someone? You must have. You must have sometimes experienced that you think of your loved one, and later, when you meet the person, he/she mention to you that he/she was also thinking about you at the same time. At times, you reach out to the phone to call a person close to you, and the person calls you at the same moment. It often happens with people in love with each other that they reach a place coincidentally and meet unexpectedly, without ever having planned to meet there.

Who orchestrates all this? It is none other than the subconscious minds of the people involved. It possesses such powers. It gets to know us every moment, whether we are asleep or awake. It understands our desires very well. That is why it fulfils them without telling us.

You don't have to go out in search of these powers; with a little effort, you just have to bring them forth from within yourself.

I had the opportunity to visit Thailand once. I went to see the Tiger Temple of Kanchanaburi. It is known as *Wat Pha Luang Ta Bua* in the local language. The temple monks had peacefully trained tigers. As a result, they were friendly with the tourists. Taking pictures with the tigers and seeing them up close was a unique experience. The temple attracts tourists from all over the world. Visitors fed tigers, walked with them, and even clicked pictures with them.

Are Thai tigers vegetarian? Or have the people who adopt them not known fear? When I inquired about this with a Buddhist monk there, he told me that they awaken the powers of their subconscious mind through various techniques taught by Lord Buddha, due to which it is not the monks who are scared of the tigers; it's the tigers that are afraid of them. They have discovered such elements of conduct, ideology, and lifestyle that eliminate fear. According to their belief, the tigers are also a part of nature, and all living beings share the same consciousness (Divine Consciousness). This belief makes them devoid of any fear of animals. All this becomes feasible only after recognizing the subconscious power of the mind.

***

Chapter 9:

Can Subconscious Powers Bring Wealth?

Before we try to find the answer to the question, it is necessary to know the basic requirements to attain wealth.

Let's start with listing a few people we consider rich. In our list, we will not include kings or others who have inherited their wealth. Whatever they possess has been inherited from their forefathers; they may have added to it or depleted it by their actions and deeds. Here is our list:

1. Dhirubhai Ambani (India)
2. Oprah Winfrey (United States)
3. Andrew Carnegie (United States)
4. Howard Schultz (United States)
5. Steve Jobs (United States)
6. Jack Ma (China)
7. J.K. Rowling (England).

There are many other wealthy people. We will draw some conclusions from the mental powers of the people mentioned in this list.

Dhirubhai Ambani was born into an ordinary family. With his insight, vision, and business acumen, he became the force behind making Reliance Industries scale great heights. It is one of the largest companies in India today.

Oprah Winfrey was also born into a poor African-American family. With her hard work and confidence, she crossed the long path to becoming the world's most famous TV host and a rich businesswoman.

Andrew Carnegie was born in 1835 in Dunfermline, Scotland. At the time of his birth, his family lived in poverty. They shifted base to America in 1848. Initially, he worked in the steel industry and later built his own company. He went on to become one of the richest men in America, donating a large part of his wealth in later years. He believed that it was the duty of the rich to use their wealth for the welfare of society. His motto was, "Make money and give it back to society."

Howard Schultz, too, spent his childhood in poverty. With hard work and determination, he transformed Starbucks from a small coffeehouse to the world's largest coffee chain. Today, he is one of the richest people in the world.

Steve Jobs was adopted soon after his birth. His adoptive parents belonged to the middle class. He went on to found Apple, which became the richest company in the world.

Jack Ma was born in a poor Chinese family. He is the founder of Alibaba, one of the world's largest e-commerce companies today. He is among the richest people in Asia.

J.K. Rowling's childhood was also marked by financial difficulties. She is the author of the *Harry Potter* series and happens to be one of the richest writers in the world.

The most unmistakable example of the powers is Jim Carrey. The Hollywood actor imagined himself as a financially successful actor when he was caught in a very challenging situation. He wrote a fake check for $10 million and kept it with him. With his hard work and instincts, he later actually earned all that money. Think about who brought all this wealth to Jim Carrey? The real owner of this wealth is his subconscious mind. It is the subconscious that searched for and found ways to solve the problems that created troubles for him. Perhaps this is why a person gives away his entire life's earnings to charity in a moment.

The first similarity among all of them is that all of them were born into poor families. Secondly, all of them reached the top through their vision, determination, and hard work. None of them had the first factor, which is vision, at birth. But all of them had within them the second – determination, the desire to achieve something. It helped them reach peaks of success. The third element was hard work.

***

Chapter 10:

Finding the Motivation to Work Hard?

How can one obtain the vision, determination, and hard work necessary to succeed? Wealth and riches of the entire world are hidden in the answer to this question.

Foresight exists covertly in our minds. Everyone has it. But it needs to be awakened. It has to be brought to the forefront and awakened. The power of the subconscious mind is needed to awaken it. Don't search for it in the outside world; search within, and you will find it very soon. Later in the book, I will describe many ways to do so.

The second prerequisite is determination. Every human being possesses determination. But many employ it in wrong pursuits. Nowadays, we see that a lot of attention is being focused on social media in searching for something completely useless. This has to be stopped, and it has to be channeled in the right direction. You have to develop determination to achieve something really big, only then will your subconscious mind do something for you.

The third and last factor is hard work. This is the element that does not naturally exist within us. If we learn the secret to it, then there is no obstacle in getting money and fame. Working hard is similar to delightfully relishing something we really like. Identify the feelings and emotions that arise in your mind when you are enjoying your favorite dish. When you face any task, try to feel the same and experience those very emotions. Don't think about why you have to do it. Don't ever think that you don't like the task. Work is always great; it should be carried out wholeheartedly.

Imagine that you work in a company and always wish that it belonged to you. In such a case, if you have one eye on the clock while working and feel that your duty is only till five or six o'clock, you can never come to own that or any similar company. But if you are engrossed in your work without paying heed to time, your subconscious mind starts creating such circumstances for you that one day you may become its owner or be able to establish a similar company. That's because it's learning from your experience, which comes in useful in your efforts to establish a company. Later on, this will be called hard work.

Sunil Vaswani, an Indian-origin entrepreneur, is today the chairman and head of Stallion Group based in Dubai. He was born in India and received his education in India and Nigeria. He is looked up to as an ideal entrepreneur in Dubai today, a feat achieved by awakening the powers of his subconscious mind, the right attitude, vision, commitment, and hard work.

He says, "Dream big and work continuously to make them come true."

Mickey Jagtiani was born in Kuwait to an Indian family. He started his career as a taxi driver. His maiden venture was a small baby products store. Today, he owns the Landmark Group, which operates in more than 20 countries. Lifestyle, Max, Home Centre, and Splash are some of its major brands.

He says, "No matter how small your beginning is, think big and keep moving forward."

***

Chapter 11:

Who is Smart — You or Your Subconscious?

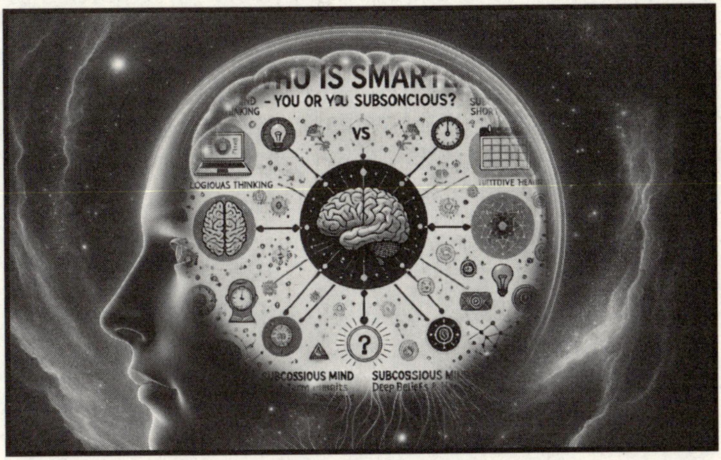

A person definitely has desires, but lacks the means to attain them. The subconscious has a complete understanding of all that the mind wishes for, but it lacks the experience to fulfill these. Only you can give this experience to it. That is why it keeps track of all your actions and deeds. It not only keeps track of the work you do but also stores in memory everything you have heard and seen. Be mindful that if you work in such a way that the outcome is not going to be good, your subconscious mind will adopt the same method the day you start your company. That is why it is said that it is important to do all your work with complete commitment.

The definition of hard work is both very complex and very clear. Everyone knows that a person building a house works very hard, but the economic returns they receive are abysmally low. Some day, a particular person from among all those laborers working hard is handpicked and made the supervisor. Have you ever deliberated about why it happens so? It is because someone notices the quality of work this particular person puts in. This particular person does not think about his comfort or anything else while he is at work. He is completely engrossed in his work and focuses only on the job he is doing. The others whom he will now be supervising over however, have a lot more to do apart from their work, which they are quite keen on doing. This was exactly the difference between Sachin Tendulkar and Vinod Kambli.

To express what hard work is in a few words: "Every time you work, consider it as your last attempt at it."

***

Chapter 12:

The Trio of Rules of Wealth

One can get wealthy by utilizing the powers of the subconscious mind. It works towards your success and prosperity by focusing your thoughts, beliefs, and mental energy. However, it is not like magic but is the result of the right attitude, hard work, and positive thinking. It is very important to know and follow three rules to get wealthy using the powers of the subconscious.

1. The Power of Thoughts

The power of the subconscious mind can convert our thoughts and beliefs about success into reality. It can make us successful. An architect never gets to see his imagination before it is completely built. He is still able to design and create buildings. This is possible because with prior experience, his subconscious mind believes that *he will be able to do it* and that *the building will not fall under any circumstances,* and that *it will last long*. That is why he can complete it. If you focus on prosperity and believe that you can achieve it, your subconscious mind motivates you in that direction.

Our thoughts directly influence our subconscious mind. It is these thoughts that create our reality. It is important to remember that our subconscious mind does not reason but accepts whatever is given to it as it is.

Positive thoughts give us confidence and motivation, while negative thoughts lead to fear and failure.

A student preparing for an exam repeatedly tells himself, "I can pass this exam. I am working hard." Such positive thoughts help his subconscious mind to make him concentrate better and believe firmly in his abilities. His confidence remains high during the exam, leading to his passing with flying colors.

Another person who wants to start a new business repeatedly keeps thinking, "This is very difficult. I will fail." Such negative thoughts scare his subconscious mind and create doubts. Instead of recognizing opportunities, the person steers clear of them and ends up failing.

2. Law of Attraction

"You become what you think," is the biggest truth about the subconscious mind. 'Faith' is its biggest power. 'Faith' is not the power of acquiring something but the power of thinking. The subconscious mind is receptive to positive thoughts and intentions and acts to turn them into reality. Many people imagine sorrows in the time to come and create future unhappiness for themselves with their own actions. Let's say you're travelling and you think, "I must attend the office tomorrow, it is very necessary to go, but I am going to be very tired by the time I reach home today…" What do you achieve by doing so? You have already told the biggest power in your body that you will be very tired tomorrow. The next day, it is going to do exactly that; you will feel exhausted and will find it difficult to focus well on work.

On the other hand, another person who accompanied you thinks, "There is an important meeting in the office tomorrow. I will work on the PPT for it as soon as I reach home. I must complete that unfinished work at once." Believe me, as soon as he reaches home, he will be working with complete dedication without feeling tired, while you will hit the bed without even changing your clothes.

3. Building Habits

Certain habits like discipline, saving, and investing are necessary for acquiring wealth. These can be developed with the help of the subconscious mind. The subconscious advises us based on what it learns from past experiences. Whether the past experience was successful or not is immaterial. Its advice is based on conclusions it has drawn. It proceeds on the basis of the person's thinking. Therefore, it is important to maintain positive thinking.

A particular task or behavior repeated time and again gets stored in the subconscious mind and becomes a habit. Tasks that are repeated often become automatic, and we don't need to consciously think about them. When you learn how to ride a bicycle, initially it is difficult. It becomes very easy with repeated practice because the subconscious mind learns and remembers it. This is why habits are difficult to change.

Initially, it is a challenge to wake up early in the morning. But then you set an alarm and prepare yourself mentally. When this is repeated for 29-30 days, it gets recorded in your subconscious mind. Your subconscious mind will then wake you up on time in the morning, even without an alarm.

Similarly, if you check your mobile repeatedly before going to sleep at night, it becomes a habit. The subconscious mind accepts it as 'natural', and then you find it difficult to resist it. If you study at the same time every day, your subconscious mind will accept it as natural in a few weeks time. Your mind will automatically get ready for studies when the time approaches.

One must repeat an action time and again to turn it into a habit. According to neuroscience, it can take 21 to 66 days to form a new habit.

Linking a new habit to old tasks makes it easier to make it a part of your behavior. For example, if you decide to meditate for 5 minutes after having tea, it becomes a part of your habits quite quickly.

Let us consider another example to understand this well. If a person addicted to smoking repeatedly says, "I am healthy, I don't need to smoke," the thought will gradually get registered in the subconscious mind, and he will give up the habit.

***

Chapter 13:

Recognizing Opportunities

Microsoft co-founders Bill Gates and Paul Allen are clear examples of the above. A company called MITS (Micro Instrumentation and Telemetry Systems) created its first microcomputer, called Altair 8800, in 1975. Suitable software (programming language) to run it was not available then. Gates and Allen proposed to MITS that they would provide the software (programming language) to run their machine. MITS accepted the proposal. Bill Gates and co-founder Paul Allen completed the deal by providing them with the language. They had made the deal based purely on their confidence and skills. This shows how advanced the positive thinking of their subconscious mind was.

"A person must persist until he finds it."

The subconscious mind helps you to identify and benefit from opportunities that you could not previously notice. Powers of the mind have a great quality of never forgetting anything. Humans tend to mix painful emotions with their memories, but the subconscious mind does not do so. It makes decisions only when it finds the situation appropriate. It does not get carried away by emotions. It knows that 'opportunity often comes in disguise.'

I remember a man who owned two belt shops in Delhi's Sadar Bazar. Though he was the owner, he entrusted his younger brother with the charge of one of the shops. The younger brother had returned from Hyderabad only a few days ago. He had become a bad alcohol addict and was also habituated to consuming drugs during his stay there. He had a shop of motor parts which used to run well, but it was now deep in debt. When the brother came to Ghaziabad, the owner's wife argued a lot with him, trying to persuade him to refrain from allowing the younger brother to manage the shop. But he hoped that his brother would give up drinking and manage the shop well.

Everything went well for some days, but then slowly his shop also started making losses. The shop had to be closed after some time. The brother realized that his decision was wrong; he should have listened to his wife and his conscience, which repeatedly tried to prevent him from doing this. But he had fallen prey to brotherly affection.

With all his previous experience, it was not as if his subconscious mind had not cautioned him from entrusting his brother with the shop. But the gentleman chose to ignore it.

He came to meet me to seek advice on how to help his brother. His wife had also accompanied him. For me, the problem was that the brother, whose mental powers needed to be awakened more than this person, had not come.

The subconscious constantly helps us to identify possibilities and opportunities through our peripheral awareness that are often outside the purview of our conscious mind. This was precisely what happened with the abovementioned businessman.

When you visualize a goal, the subconscious mind starts to accept it as your reality. For example, if you are looking for a job, the subconscious mind will help you focus on networking opportunities and jobs that might otherwise go unnoticed. It draws your attention to opportunities that can take you closer to your goal. Your subconscious mind determines the direction of your focus.

If you're an entrepreneur looking for business partnerships, your subconscious mind will prioritize the conversations, people, and networking opportunities most conducive to your search. If you are attending a social event, your subconscious mind attracts you to people who can be useful for your business.

If you want to learn a skill to advance in your career, the subconscious mind focuses on courses, seminars, and online content that can meet your needs.

You may suddenly come across advertisements, articles, or people related to that skill.

If your focus is on financial freedom, your subconscious mind helps you identify investment opportunities, business ideas, and savings plans.

If you value positive and honest relationships, your subconscious mind will help you identify people who might be good for you. It helps you focus on signs and behaviors that will lead you to a good relationship.

You should always remember that your subconscious mind is conscious every moment, even if you forget the purpose of your life.

Whatever you repeatedly input into your subconscious mind becomes your reality.

***

Chapter 14:

How Does the Subconscious Mind Operate?

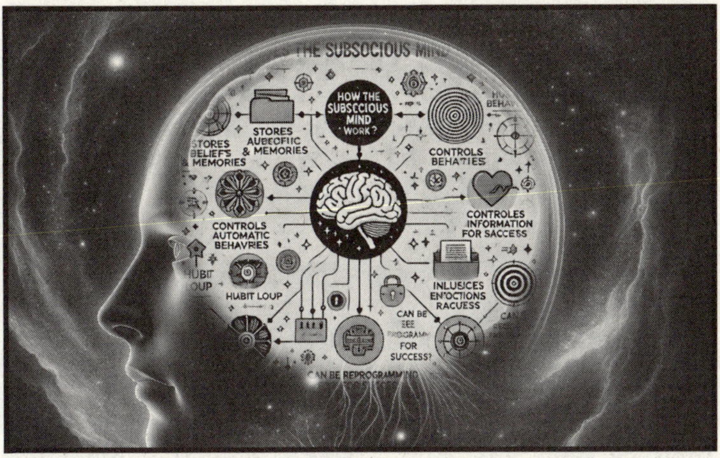

The subconscious mind is the database manager of our body. It amasses all the intangible experiences and feelings within us. It shapes and molds our beliefs and thoughts. Whatever we repeatedly think or feel gets deeply etched in the subconscious mind. This database influences our behavior. We are under the illusion that we are the doers, but in reality, with the power of the subconscious, it is our previous experiences that are doing everything.

If a person imagines that he will have a fever when he gets drenched in the rain, the subconscious mind draws on some past experience, and the person really gets sick. Because it had happened before, it's not necessary that it should happen again. It happens so even though it was not supposed to happen in the same manner this time, because of past experience. Similarly, if one feels and starts imagining that he is going to get burnt or get injured in an accident, then it will start creating circumstances so that it actually happens because it starts feeling that those thoughts are right.

Deep emotions and experiences, like childhood experiences of fear or happiness, are strongly imprinted on it. A person's daily routine, like getting up in the morning, brushing teeth, or their reaction to a particular situation, is governed by the subconscious mind. Therefore, if you develop positive habits, the subconscious mind makes them a part of your life.

Though we are not consciously aware of it, it is the subconscious that often drives our decisions. This is the first of the hidden powers of the subconscious mind. We can call it the intangible power of decision-making.

Some people who realize this secret start deceiving their subconscious mind. They know that whatever the subconscious mind wants will mostly happen. Therefore, they force it to do what they want. They continuously start thinking about what they want to happen. For example, if Sachin in his youth had not dreamt that he would become one of the best cricket players in the world one day, the circumstances around him would not have been created the way they were. Vinod, on the other hand, started thinking that he had conquered the world and was a hero, so there was no harm in trying a hand at being the villain. This is why he tried his luck in films, clubs, etc. It is also important to state here that there is another hidden power in action. We can call it the power of karma. We will discuss it later.

The subconscious mind acts as a great guide in our lives. It can make or break our aspirations. It works according to the instructions we give it. If we think of instructions indicating the heights of achievements, that's where it takes us. If we think of instructions depicting depths of misfortune, it takes us far away from success. This is its second power, the ability to direct.

Some of you might remember that people of the past boasted of an excellent memory. They could remember the phone numbers and addresses of many people. But ever since we have become dependent on mobile phones, our memory has decreased. Even before we try to remember something, we tell our mind to look it up on the mobile. The actual power to remember is the same; it has not decreased.

I have written a book about my life. When I started writing it, I did not remember much. I never had a very good memory. It took me ten years, but I completed my autobiography, *Inventing Dreams.* As I started writing the book, my subconscious displayed every incident of my life vividly like a movie for me.

The subconscious mind is an invisible controller of our lives. It stores our thoughts and beliefs and constantly works to transform them into our reality.

***

Chapter 15:

Can the Subconscious be the Fountainhead of Youth?

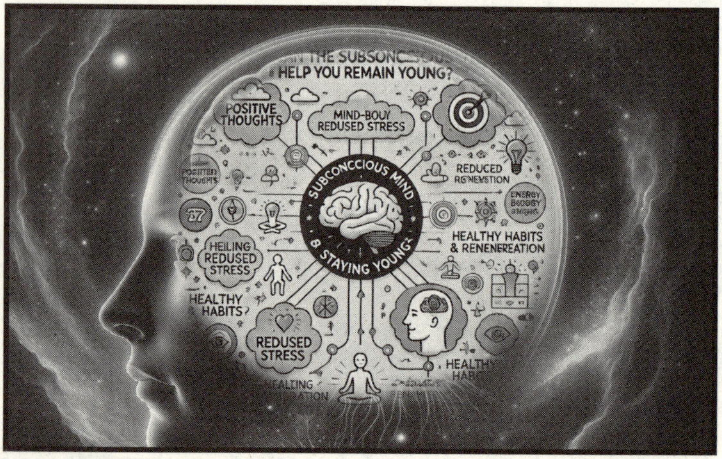

Breathing is essential to human life, or for that matter, every living creature on the earth. It is said that plants and trees also breathe. Who controls breathing? How does it take place?

If one's heart is beating, then we know that the person is breathing, he has life in his body, and then he is said to be alive.

It is the subconscious that controls our breathing. It controls the automatic processes of our body. It gives us the awareness of our heartbeat. If someone is unwell and they go to the doctor, the doctor uses a stethoscope to listen to the person's heartbeat to arrive at a diagnosis.

When the doctor diagnoses a disease in the body based on the heartbeat, and we accept that some power of our subconscious mind is controlling it, we will have to accept that this is its third intangible power. If someone refuses to believe in it, it doesn't matter, as no one can say that they can control the heartbeat. When this subconscious power in someone's mind dies and the person is still alive, it means that he is dependent on some medical machinery or a ventilator. Life can leave his body at any moment.

It is necessary that our thoughts, emotions, and mental state should remain conducive to improving the energy, enthusiasm, and health of our body. The positive signals going to the body through the subconscious mind improve energy, enthusiasm, and health. These signals work at the cellular level, which improves the skin, energy, and health of the body. The power of the subconscious mind plays an important role in remaining young and energetic.

With positive thinking, anyone can remain young. If your mind accepts that you are young, you are not old, then the heart cannot become sick without any reason. Growing old with time is a different phenomenon. But being ill often is due to the absence or lack of strength of the mind.

The implication and conclusion of this discussion is that if our heart is healthy and young, then we are also young. We can believe that it helps to be young. If one thinks that he is old, it will make him old and sick. On the other hand, believing that one is young will make one remain youthful. That's because the invisible power of the mind will convert whatever we think into reality.

When the mind is calm and balanced, the subconscious mind protects the body from the damage caused by stress, such as wrinkles, fatigue, and diseases. It reduces the level of stress hormones like cortisol in the body, making it feel more youthful. The subconscious mind speeds up the process of regeneration of the body, which removes old cells and creates new cells in the body. If you imagine your skin, energy, and body being healthy and glowing every day, it will keep regenerating the cells in the body better and faster.

***

Chapter 16:

Who Can Be Successful?

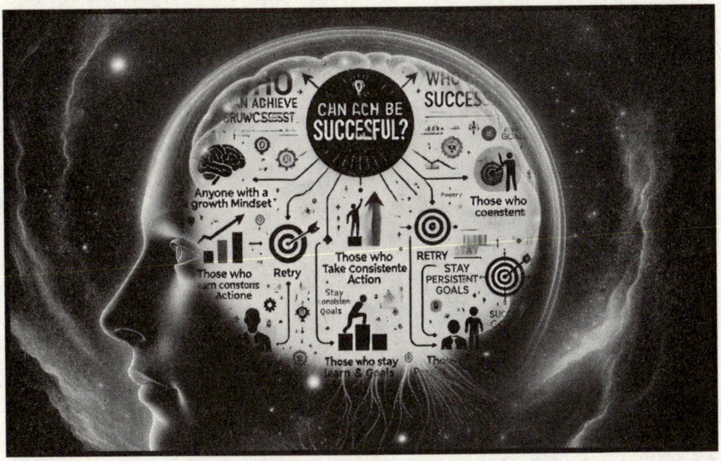

Our mind works based on emotions and faith rather than logic. Right from childhood, the subconscious mind stores everything that happens. It has an infinite memory. All the information is stored with it.

A human being is imaginative from birth. While it is the source of inspiration, it can also be his biggest weakness. Sometimes, reliance on the power of imagination can ruin lives. I know a person whose father named him Harshvardhan after the famous

King. On his birth, an astrologer had predicted that the child's horoscope showed that he had all the qualities befitting a king. The father hoped that the boy would grow up to become a king in stature, and he started raising him with this mindset. His life, unfortunately, was short, and he passed away early. But the thought had been planted firmly into that child. Harshvardhan also grew up thinking the same. He could have become a king, but he never worked hard. With time, he lost hope, but it was too late by then. He did small odd jobs at many places, but could never rise up, and he got lost in oblivion one day. Long ago, I saw him by the road in a very pitiful condition.

He had big thoughts, but failed to awaken the power of his subconscious mind. This was because he neither studied suitably to become a king nor did he practice yoga, meditation, or penance, which could have awakened those powers. That is why he could not live the life that was granted to him.

Our mind works only in the present. It does not understand the past and the future; it reacts to the signals given to it. Therefore, instead of thinking about failures in the past, we should think about when we succeeded. One should always think, "I will definitely succeed." Every task should be performed with this thought. This positive thinking is the fourth power of the subconscious. Directing it with positive thoughts can bring about big changes in life. Repeating positive sentences like "I am successful," and "I can do this very easily" increases self-confidence, and success can also be achieved through this.

***

Chapter 17:

Contribution of the Subconscious in Being Healthy

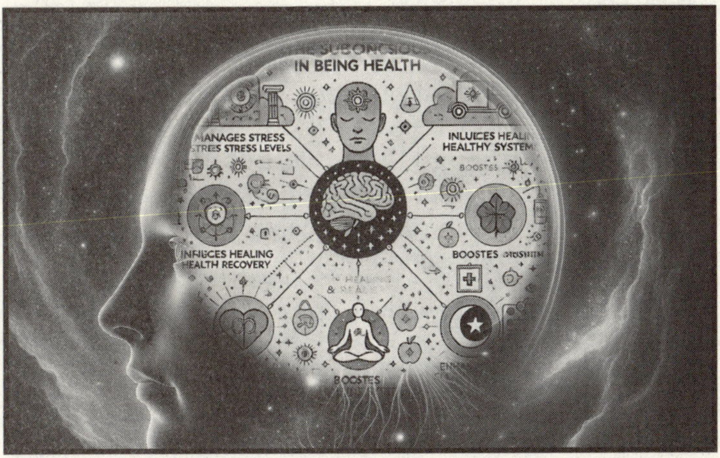

The tradition of treating people using the power of their subconscious mind has existed since the *Vedic* period in India and also all over the world. Its history can be traced back to antiquity. Its success can be gauged from the fact that many institutes devoted to healing through the subconscious have been established in the world as well as in India. Many people from abroad come to India to benefit from it. Even today, it is applied in myriad different ways. Treatment using the power of the subconscious mind is usually administered through psychotherapy, meditation, yoga, *pranayama,* and positive thinking. It is used successfully not only to treat mental problems but also physical ailments.

One of such institutes, the Ramamani Iyengar Memorial Yoga Institute, is located in Pune. Here, diseases are treated by activating the powers of the subconscious mind.

At the Art of Living *Ashram,* located in Bangalore, mental stress and anxiety are relieved by awakening these powers. Breathing techniques are taught using these powers.

Vipassana Meditation Center, located in Igatpuri, Maharashtra, also teaches how to increase self-consciousness through the powers of the subconscious mind. This helps in cleansing the subconscious mind over and over again, and it then keeps opening new doors for you every moment.

The Kerala Ayurveda Centre, established in 2004 by Dr. Mahendra Sharma, is located in Jaipur. Contrary to the name, it is not located in the state of Kerala. This institute also teaches the methods of awakening the powers of the mind, and they explain how one can heal oneself and stay young by using these powers.

Jindal Naturecare Institute and the National Institute of Mental Health and Neurosciences in Bangalore also treat physical ailments through yoga, positive thinking, and meditation.

Apart from all these, AIIMS and Self-Healing Institute of Delhi, Isha Foundation of Coimbatore, many centers of Ramakrishna Foundation, and the Indian Society of Clinical Hypnosis, Mumbai, use techniques like hypnotherapy to reprogram the subconscious mind through self-awareness. All these use spirituality and meditation to give a positive direction to the subconscious mind. Their message to us is that by awakening the latent powers in our bodies, we can be successful and healthy.

***

Chapter 18:

Tantra for Awakening the Subconscious

Our sages and saints were the first in the world to recognize these dormant powers. To begin with, they believed that a human being can achieve anything; whether it is knowledge, the power to fight diseases, or even the revelation of the creator of this universe—nothing is beyond us. The technique, means, effort, and intellect to know all this very much exists within us, hidden in the subconscious. They had also discovered the means to activate these glands. Some of these techniques are called *Tantra*. *Tantra* is nothing but a method of meditation. Though it has its origins in meditation, the ways of deploying it are different.

According to Freud, the dreams and Freudian slips that anyone can witness give us a glimpse into the 'subconscious mind'. Sometimes, it's thinking is so deep that it becomes our dreams.

In those times, many centers were established to understand the subconscious mind. Very little information or proof about them is available now. Some new centers were also established to propagate the use of *tantric* power.

The city of Varanasi in Uttar Pradesh is the foremost among such centers established to awaken and propagate knowledge of the powers of the subconscious mind. Many mental and physical problems are successfully treated in the city using the subconscious mind through many *Siddha* and *Tantric* traditions.

Osho International Meditation Resort in Pune and the Sathya Sai Baba *Ashram* in Puttaparthi, Andhra Pradesh, are also known for developing self-confidence and positive thinking.

The third such seat is the Kamakhya temple situated in Assam. Here also, ancient *tantric* methods are applied to awaken the subconscious mind and the energy centers in the body. An important factor to note here is that the location is of major significance for awakening the dormant powers of our body. Where you do all this has a great impact. How much time it will take to awaken them is also determined by the powers of the place. Some people are aware of this, and they deliberate a lot beforehand to choose the appropriate place for it.

That is the reason Steve Jobs came to India and visited the Himalayan region, Haridwar, Rishikesh, and Varanasi. Mountains, a peaceful corner in one's own home, *Siddha Peeths*, temple complexes, peepal or banyan trees, and natural caves are the best places for this.

These powers can also be called *Prana* energy. We acquire this energy only after awakening these powers. It may be called by different names across the world, but the purpose is the same—to awaken and benefit from it.

This power is known as *Chi* in China, *Zen* in Japan, Mindfulness in America, *Sila Podsoznania* in Russia, *Ouvrir de l* in France, *Kraft des Unterbewusstsein* in Germany, *Jamjae Uishik-Ui Him* in Korea, *Phlang Chit Tai Sammanuk* in Thailand, *Dynami tou Iposiniditu* in Greece, *Quwwat al-Aql al-B'tin* in Arab countries, and *Potere del Subconsciou* in Italy.

What we can conclude from this is that the whole world has accepted that these powers exist and are useful. Of all these powers, the deepest and most powerful power humans have is the mental power of consciousness. It is also called subconscious power.

***

Chapter 19:

Psychological Therapy

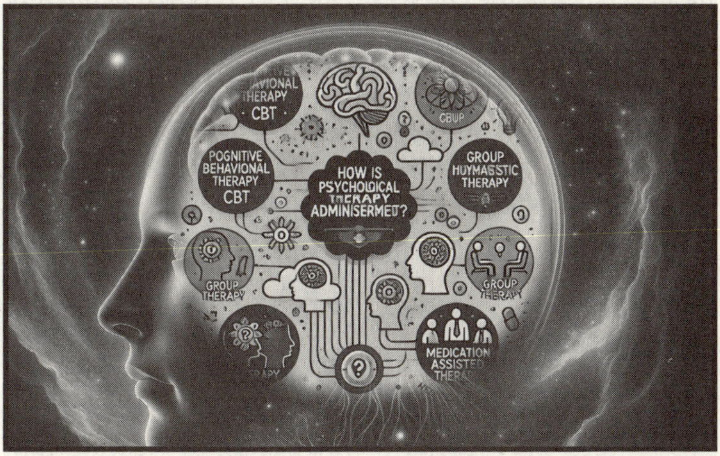

Here are some of the problems that every person in this world, whether they lived in the past or in modern times, has faced at some time or the other:

1. Stress and anxiety
2. Depression and negative thinking
3. Insomnia
4. Phobias and fears
5. Lack of self-confidence

6. High blood pressure and heart disease (partially)
7. Treatment of addictions (e.g., quitting smoking).

Irrespective of whether we call them aspects of life or problems, everyone has encountered these at some point or other in their lives. A good part of a person's life is invested in trying to eliminate them. But what people fail to realize is that these are actually not the problems at all. They are the causes created by them. It is not any treatment but mental power that is needed to get rid of them. A person has the power within themselves, but out of ignorance, they look for it in the outside world. He keeps looking for a cure for these problems at medical centers, with astrologers or accomplished sages, or sometimes by causing pain to himself.

All he needs to do is think that he is alright, nothing is wrong with him, and he is not going to die. A man came to me once. The doctor had diagnosed him as a patient with insomnia. I asked about his routine, and after getting the information, gave him a powdered formulation to help him sleep. I told him to try to sleep and to take the powder before sleeping, assuring him that he would sleep well.

He was happy when he came in the morning. When I enquired with him about the night, he happily told me that he had slept really well the previous night. I sent him back, asking him to sleep without taking any medicines that day.

Believe it or not, my wife is my witness that I had told her to crush a simple, small common fever tablet and fill it in a sachet. The insomnia patient could sleep well because of that.

While taking the medicine, the subconscious mind of that person must have been telling him repeatedly that he would sleep well at night as he was taking sleeping medicine. So he slept well. Now you will realize how the power of the subconscious mind works instantly and effectively. The power of his subconscious was not even awakened. Still, it worked perfectly. The great psychoanalyst Freud has also explained this. He calls it the Placebo Effect. When a person is made to believe that he is being given a medicine (although it is fake), his body responds positively.

This illustrates the power of the subconscious mind and that beliefs and mindset can affect our physical health.

You must have heard that many who want to quit smoking have been successful after some time by using plain smoking cigarettes that emit smoke instead of actual tobacco cigarettes. One word almost always used for such cases is 'Will Power'. Have you ever thought about what it is? It is not any organ in our body. It is the power of the subconscious mind. The willpower of many people is awakened from birth, and some people awaken it through practice.

***

Chapter 20:

Are These Powers Infinite?

Once upon a time, there lived a very pious queen. She had four sons. The king suddenly passed away one day. A monk came to the palace at the time of the funeral and imparted a lot of true knowledge about life to the queen. He advised the queen that she should ensure such education for her sons that they would attain salvation in that life itself.

The queen started educating all the princes under her personal care. They were mostly taught about religion and the truth of the soul. The youngest prince was a lot younger than his other brothers. He could not, therefore, at his tender young age, understand that knowledge.

After some time, all three princes became ascetics, renouncing the physical world and the kingdom and its luxuries. After a passage of time, the queen handed over the kingdom to the young prince. As time passed, the queen was about to breathe her last. At that time, the queen handed over a letter to the king, her youngest son, and asked him to open it when he started getting old.

In due time, the king opened the letter. "Life is an illusion, Brahma is the only truth, spend the rest of your life in the quest for truth. Only the soul is immortal; it never dies," was the message written in it.

Tears rolled down the prince's eyes. He donated his entire kingdom and became a monk.

The queen knew very well that the powers of her children's subconscious minds would make them whatever she would teach their subconscious minds. So tell your mind what you want to become or get, and that will happen.

***

Chapter 21:

Willpower — The Mightiest Power

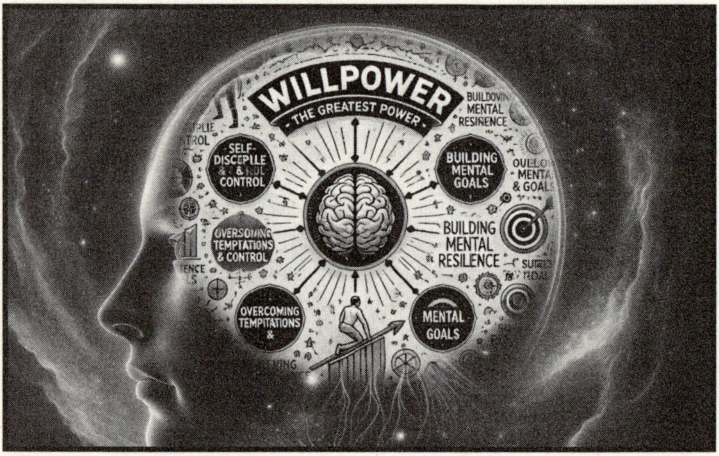

Willpower is critical in every aspect of life. It encourages us to reach our goals and keeps us going during difficulties. It can also be called the first and the fourth power of the subconscious mind. Willpower can be fortified through regular practice, discipline, and positive thinking. Willpower means controlling oneself and moving firmly towards the goal even while facing difficult situations. It is a form of mental strength and self-control; its foundation is nothing but positivity.

If a person repeatedly says, "I will become rich," or "I am going to be rich," it's impossible that they will actually get rich, even if they keep doing so throughout their life. But if someone thinks, "I am rich," "I am rich," they are bound to become rich. The difference between the two is subtle. The first person's statements imply that "I am poor right now, I am not wealthy, and I should become rich." His subconscious will accept this first statement – "I am poor and will start working on it." It will not pay any attention to anything else. But as far as the other person is concerned, it hears only one thing – "I am rich, I am wealthy," again and again. So, it will get busy making that happen. It does not need anything else. That is why it is said that one should not think too intelligently; otherwise, the subconscious will get involved in it, and the result will be the opposite of what was desired.

Willpower is the invincible strength in our body that has helped many people throughout history succeed despite great difficulties. There are many who not only changed their own circumstances with their willpower, but also became an inspiration for others.

***

Chapter 22:

Overcoming Nature with the Subconscious

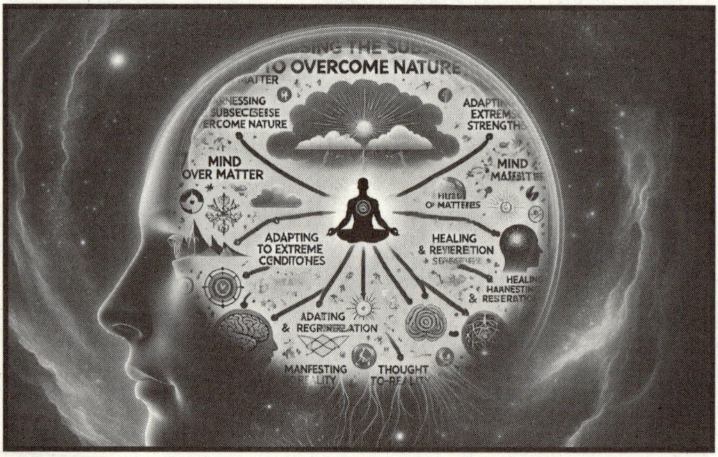

The very first name that comes to our minds when we think of overcoming physical problems through willpower is that of Stephen Hawking. Hawkins suffered from motor neuron disease (ALS) at the age of 21, rendering most of his body inactive. Such was his willpower that he did not let his illness be an impediment in the way of his purpose and made a stellar contribution to cosmology. His book, *A Brief History of Time*, brought him international fame.

The second example is Helen Keller. She lost her sense of hearing and sight in early childhood. Despite this, she overcame her disability, received a comprehensive education, and became a great writer, demonstrating her willpower. She went on to do a lot of work for the rights of the disabled across the world.

Thomas Edison, the great inventor, is also a classic example. While studying in school, Edison was branded slow and useless. But he continued progressing with strong willpower. He suffered 1000 failures before inventing the bulb. But he did not accept defeat. Edison made his failures a means of learning and finally invented the bulb. His paradigm was, "I did not fail; I found 1000 ways that did not work." Strong willpower is an enormous power. No other sentence can describe it better. Willpower gives us the strength to go beyond our limits and make the impossible (for those who know what it means) possible.

We know that the physical and mental capacities of our bodies diminish over time. Our subconscious mind even has the ability to reduce or change the impact of these rules. The above examples prove it. The subconscious mind, if trained properly, can overcome boundaries and turn the impossible into possible. It motivates the mind to rise above natural barriers.

Many scientific and medical studies show that positive thinking and instructions from the subconscious mind can help the body in healing. According to the Placebo Effect propounded by Freud, when a person believes they are taking medicine, their body starts recovering.

Louise Hay, a spiritual teacher and motivational speaker from the United States, also healed herself from a serious illness using her subconscious mind and inspired millions to heal themselves. In her extremely famous book *You Can Heal Your Life,* she explains how the thoughts and beliefs of our subconscious mind have a profound impact on our health and lives. The book has been translated into more than 30 languages and millions of people across the world have read it.

***

Chapter 23:

Subconscious — A Great Help in Solving Complex Problems

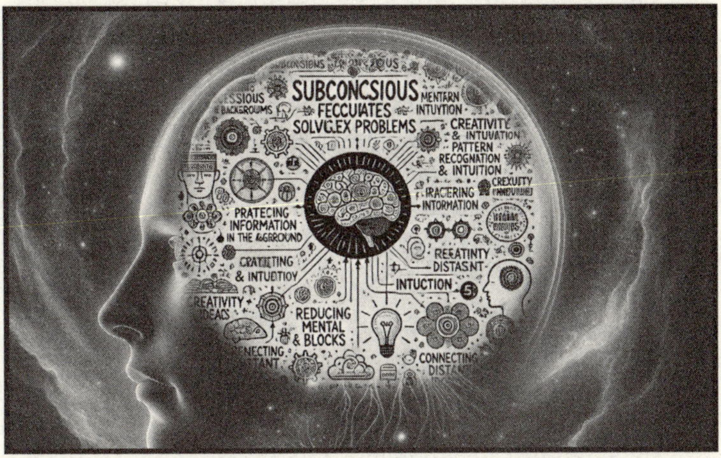

Neuroplasticity of the brain is a hidden power in the mind of every human being. It is the scientific name of the ability to learn new habits and thoughts. The same can be instrumental in reprogramming the subconscious mind by adopting and practicing positive thoughts. It can be awakened easily in early childhood. This is why a child can learn even the most difficult of languages at the age of 5 to 6 years very easily. The number just doesn't matter. The number of languages that can be learnt by a child has no limit because the brain's neuroplasticity is very active at this age.

I know a person who taught six languages to his four children at his home in Chicago. He invited language experts from China and India to stay with them to teach the children Chinese and Hindi. The family went to France and Italy and lived there. That's how they learnt French and Italian. Due to very little awareness about neuroplasticity, very few people in India put it to use.

The scientific name of another power of the subconscious is Sleep Learning. It's not just the mind that can absorb new information by awakening this power; research has shown that the body also acquires it. Sleep Learning, or Hypnopedia, is the process through which a person absorbs information during sleep. This phenomenon is based on the fact that our subconscious mind is active even while we sleep and can process new information.

The story of Abhimanyu cited in the Hindu epic of the *Mahabharata* is a great example of this. His father, Arjun, had narrated a secret to his mother, Subhadra, when she was pregnant. Subhadra, however, heard it only partially because she fell asleep. So, Arjun, his father also went to sleep. Abhimanyu was born in due course. Then came a day when young Abhimanyu needed to use the knowledge he had heard when he was in the womb. History is witness that young Abhimanyu used that secret knowledge word by word to the extent his mother had heard it. Later, however, his incomplete knowledge resulted in his death.

There can be no greater example of the fact that the power of our subconscious mind can help solve complex problems than that of Abhimanyu.

I have often heard many parents say that their child was fast asleep at night when they discussed something, but the child started telling them about the same things or started doing them after it woke up in the morning. It is the 'sleep learning' power of the child's subconscious mind that is behind this.

As we sleep, our brain passes through various stages, which affect the learning process. The first stage is REM (Rapid Eye Movement) Sleep. A person dreams in this stage, but the brain is less receptive to learning. The second stage is NREM (Non-Rapid Eye Movement) Sleep. This can be considered particularly deep sleep. The subconscious mind processes and preserves the information received by the brain during this phase.

The purpose of sleep learning is to give new information or knowledge to the subconscious mind during sleep. A person should repeatedly listen to an audio recording (such as words, phrases, or motivational thoughts) while sleeping for this. This information is then transferred to the brain and recorded subconsciously in the mind. It can be recalled more easily after waking up. Listening to new words and phrases during sleep can help improve vocabulary.

Positive messages reach deep into the subconscious mind and can influence a person's behavior in a positive direction.

***

Chapter 24:

Ensuring the Subconscious is Active As We Sleep

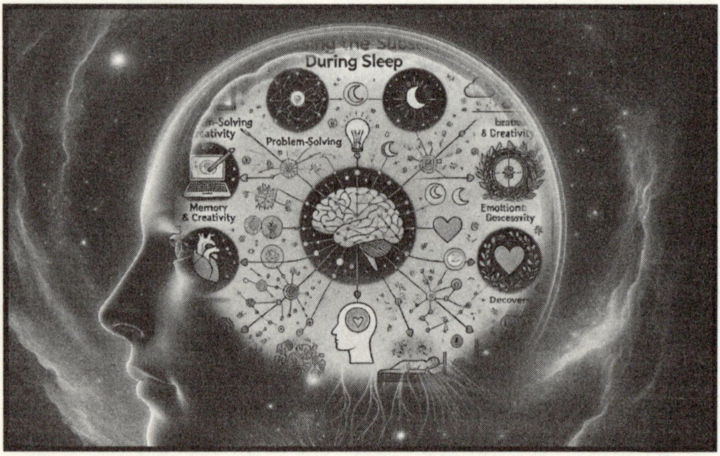

Thomas Edison tried to keep his mind 'active' even while he slept, when he was working on his inventions. He would focus on a particular problem before going to sleep and work on finding a solution while sleeping.

Albert Einstein believed that the brain works on ideas left unfinished during waking hours while we sleep. He employed sleep learning to understand parts of his Theory of Relativity. He would 'rest' his brain during sleep and get solutions to complex problems after waking up.

Leonardo da Vinci also used sleep learning for his creative projects and engineering designs. He adopted a 'polyphasic sleep' pattern, in which the brain remains active even during short sleep intervals. He used to repeatedly revise information related to his art or design before going to sleep.

The famous artist Salvador Dali used sleep learning to develop ideas in his dreams in a semi-sleep state. He would think about his paintings before sleeping and paint the ideas after waking up.

The great mathematician and scientist John von Neumann also used to train his brain to solve complex mathematical problems during sleep; he would keep repeating mathematical equations before sleeping. He could find the solution to all his problems on waking up.

Franklin D. Roosevelt, Jim Kwik, and Oprah Winfrey are also said to have used sleep learning for self-improvement and motivation.

Elon Musk, the CEO of Tesla and SpaceX, has also used the 'productive rest' technique during sleep time.

***

Chapter 25:

Science Behind the Subconscious

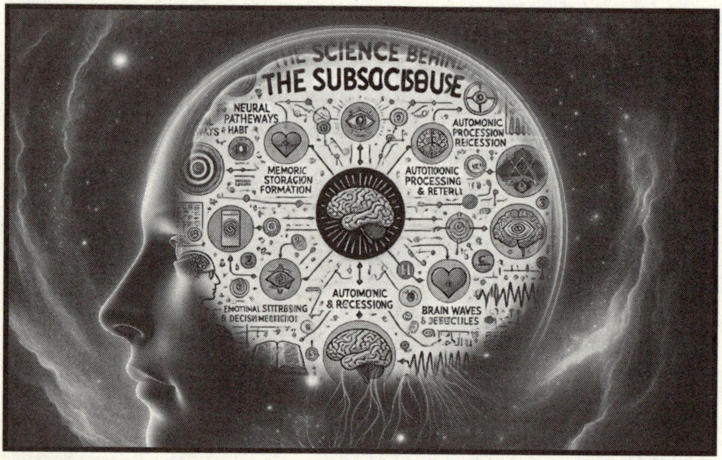

According to neuroscience, the subconscious mind controls about 90% of the brain's activities. Freud calls this the 'Iceberg Model.' It completely affects our thoughts, feelings, and behavior. Scientists, therefore, also call it the 'Automatic Brain.' The scientific aspects of the power of the subconscious mind are related to the study of the brain, neuroscience, psychology, and human behavior. This definition helps us understand how the subconscious mind operates and affects our thoughts, feelings, and decisions.

The most salient feature of the subconscious mind is that it works automatically; we don't have to make any special effort for it to work. Once awakened, it remains alert all the time. It is a treasure trove of experience. It keeps on storing our memories, habits, and emotions.

Many people want to acquire wealth and get rich. But then quite often, they look at others and say, "What's the big deal about money?" Just imagine how their subconscious mind will think... "What's the big deal about the desire to get rich? What's there in wealth?" Therefore, we must be extremely careful about our thoughts about our desires. The subconscious does not like a state of dilemma. You will get clear and good results only when you have absolute faith and abundant willpower.

In scientific parlance, the Limbic System controls our emotions and memories. The mind's responses to fear and danger are stored in the amygdala. The hippocampus stores our long-term memories. It is the hippocampus, which is called the automatic brain. It also controls automatic functions like breathing, maintaining heartbeats, muscle reactions, etc. It is the subconscious mind behind all this.

***

Chapter 26:

Exorcizing Mother's 'Spirit'

Once, a man came to me with a peculiar problem. He used to work as a manager in a bank in Janakpuri, Delhi. He had a good job and had inherited a nice house. He was now the sole owner of that house. His cup was filled to the brim. But he was badly addicted to alcohol. He claimed that he saw the cadaver of his late mother every moment.

After he came to meet me, I was convinced that he did not resort to alcohol of his own accord. I tried to look into what weighed on his mind and realized that his mother had passed away some 7-8 years ago.

It was just after that that he had started drinking due to an inability to sleep. He had to go to the bank in the morning, but he could not sleep at night. He could sleep only after drinking alcohol.

He now wanted to give up alcohol completely. On further investigation, I came to know that he saw his late mother all the time. This petrified him. He could somehow manage the time spent in the bank, but he could not handle it while at home. As a result, he took refuge in alcohol.

On prodding a little more, I discovered that he was drunk the day his mother breathed her last and at the time he cremated her. Ever since then, he started fearing that his mother would take him along with her to punish him for that sin. He could not get over the fear, and it kept him terrified all the time.

I could gauge that the anxiety had seeped very deep into his subconscious. It needed to be done away with. When I enquired further with him, he told me that his mother would ask him for some makeup items, a red *sari,* and a bed.

I told him to buy all those things. I specifically asked him to buy all the stuff from Haridwar. I advised him to give away all the objects except the red *sari*, along with his mother, whom he could always see by his side, to some priest there. He was to bring the red *sari* back to Delhi and call me.

He trusted me fully and followed my instructions to the 't'. After a few days, I received his call informing me that he had done exactly as I had instructed and was now back in Delhi with that red *sari*. He wanted to know what was to be done next.

I asked him if his mother was still there with him. He replied in the affirmative. She was now asking him why he had given all the things to the priest there, instead of giving them to her, he said. She was also telling him to at least give the *sari* to her.

I sensed that his subconscious mind had understood what I had hinted at. I told him, "Take that *sari* and go to Tilak Nagar (in Delhi) and offer it to the goddess Santoshi *Mata* at the hands of the temple priest. Your mother will leave you and sit in that temple to take that *sari*. She will never come to you again."

He did the same. After a few days, he came to me with sweets. He had not had a drop of alcohol till that day. He and his wife were overjoyed. His wife told me that after coming back from the temple, he had not consumed alcohol even once, nor had he asked for it. She said that in fact, he was now scared of alcohol. I laughed.

The only purpose behind sharing this story is to share with the readers that our subconscious mind can even bring people from the dead to meet us. It is so very powerful. This incident is absolutely true.

***

Chapter 27:

Where's the Subconscious' Storehouse?

The subconscious mind has unlimited data storage to accumulate a lot and keep it carefully. It is the huge 'hard drive' of the brain. All a person's experiences from childhood to the present day are collected and stored there by the subconscious. It repeatedly ponders over them, influencing our decisions and reactions, and making us feel emotions like fear, happiness, and pain. It is important to note here that positive and negative biases have an enduring impact on our minds. Positive thoughts permanently imprinted in our subconscious are conducive to achieving success. Negative thoughts, on the other hand, become the reason for fear and failure.

Sigmund Freud, considered the father of psychoanalysis, was endowed with a complex and unique personality. He was known for his revolutionary thinking and analytical approach. He was the first to try to understand human psychology and emotions in depth. He pioneered new concepts such as the id, ego, and superego, where he believed the subconscious mind to be residing. However, his theories were quite unlike the traditional views and were often controversial. He raised many questions about the human brain and behavior and invented new methods to find answers to them. All of them were used to unravel the subconscious mind. Id, ego, and superego are created from the data stored by the subconscious mind. It may be good sometimes or bad at times. But think about who provides data to the subconscious? It's none other than you. That is why 'positive thinking' is repeated so often.

What is surprising is that, though Freud knew that consuming cigars or tobacco could cause cancer, he did not stop smoking cigars and eventually developed mouth cancer. Freud said goodbye to the world, trying to define the human mind, pioneering a new way of looking at psychological patients, and giving new dimensions to their treatment.

All his psychological theories fade away at this point because the invisible power people call by names like *Bhagwan*, *Ishwar*, *Allah*, Jesus Christ, *Baba Guru Nanak,* or God, etc., is in command here.

"Doors closed by *karma* never open again."

The disease, which was going to bring his death due to cigar smoking, was predetermined; he could not have stopped it. The conscious power of the subconscious mind has no effect on this; it is only the latent power that works.

***

Chapter 28:

One Reason for Success and A Hundred for Failure

You must have often heard many people reminisce about things like, "I would have been successful had I had a little more money," "If only my relatives were not nice enough to help me," "Alas! I was about to win a lottery, but I lost my ticket," "If I had not sold my plot, it would have been worth crores of rupees today," "If my parents had educated me properly, I would also have been a successful man today," in the later years of their life. One finds numerous factors to blame and reasons to hide behind for failures suffered.

But if someone asks a great person how they achieved all that they did, they will have only one answer. They will say, "I just worked hard relentlessly." They are not likely to have much to say about how they reached where they are. It is not that they don't want to share it lest someone else follow them and achieve the same stature. It is only because their sole focus while working was on 'becoming successful.' The unsuccessful keep thinking about one or the other thing they lack or grumble about why they have to do such lowly tasks when they actually long to be great.

Once, a person left a lit lamp and left for someplace else to finish a certain assignment. Another man came in a while and saw many unlit lamps lying around. He noticed the lighted lamp and felt inspired to light other lamps. He started lighting the unlit lamps with the help of the one lamp that was lit. He lit hundreds of lamps. The first person returned in a short while. He asked the other person which one was his lamp. The other person, shaking his head, said that he had no idea.

The purpose of sharing this anecdote with you is that you should try lighting the lamp of just one of the powers of your subconscious mind. In a very short time, you will forget that you were wandering in the darkness in search of light. You will discover so many powers activated within you that it will be impossible to identify which power you had awakened first. Keep reading the deep secrets mentioned in this book with continued concentration, and then your mind will be lit with the bright light of enthusiasm.

***

Chapter 29:

Success Awaits at the Next Corner

A person who lives in America has innovated many products. He said that he got an invite from Microsoft once to present his products to them. He informed me that his team selected five of his company's products for the meeting. Just as he was leaving for the meeting, he picked up another small product to demonstrate it to Microsoft. In the end, Microsoft bought his company for a good price because of that particular product.

'Opportunities knock on the back door at any time.'

Poverty can be an obstacle in life, but it can be overcome with willpower, hard work, and determination. The success of many such people is proof that no matter what the circumstances, anyone can make their dreams come true with the right attitude and hard work.

Many people whine about how they worked hard all their lives, and put in a lot of effort, but did not achieve success. What work requires is honesty within oneself and not labor. If one follows the advice of others from time to time and does not listen to one's own subconscious, this is inevitable. One does not pay heed when the subconscious says that one should not harm anyone, one ignores it when it says that one should spend only as per one's capacity and ends up spending as if there's no tomorrow, when the subconscious cautions that a promise made to someone in business should always be fulfilled so that they will be supportive when needed, one does not listen even then; one turns a deaf ear to it when it says, "what you are doing to show off to others will cause problems in the future." When the subconscious advises to try to complete something once again, one ignores that, too.

Such people don't know that "success was waiting just at the next corner where they left off."

***

Chapter 30:

How to Make the Best of the Subconscious Mind

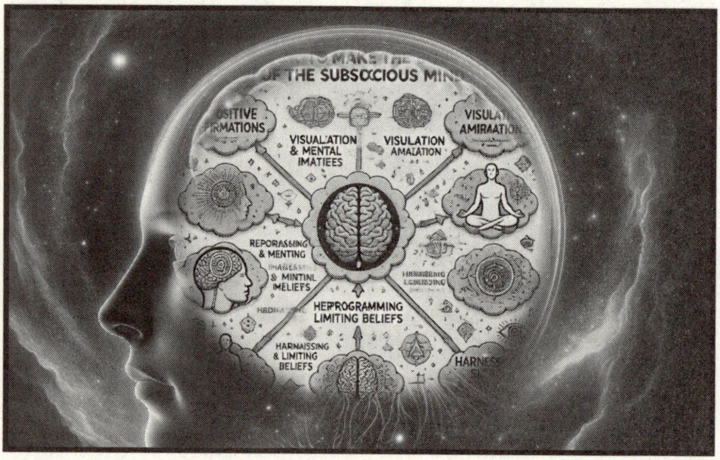

Here are a few points that are the basis of all theories. We undoubtedly need wisdom that can improve our lives and make us successful and wealthy. The whole background so far has been given only because our mind and conscience needed to start to believe that something like this is possible before we proceed.

"I also possess the mightiest power in the world."

It will be useless to proceed unless one has accepted it first. The whole structure depends on what our heart, conscience, or mind believes that it would be possible. Imagine that you are sitting on the mat spread out there with faith that it is possible, and these powers will emerge only then. It definitely happens, it has happened in the past, and will happen again.

Positive Thinking and Faith

Convince yourself that you can earn money. Frequently repeat "I am financially prosperous" in your mind. Use many such affirmations. These will eliminate your negative thinking and prepare your mind for success. You must have heard about many yogis living in the Himalayas in temperatures ranging from -20°C to -40°C, in exceeding cold and difficult conditions. What is it that they have? It is only the power of their subconscious mind that says, "It is not cold, my body is not feeling cold." Yoga, meditation, and techniques like '*Tummo* Meditation' are at an advanced level compared to this. To begin with, it is necessary to believe that it is possible.

Writing is a way to crystallize the feelings and thoughts of the subconscious mind. Adopt free writing – write whatever comes to your mind without a break. This also helps in bringing out the powers of the subconscious mind.

***

Chapter 31:

Power of Visualization

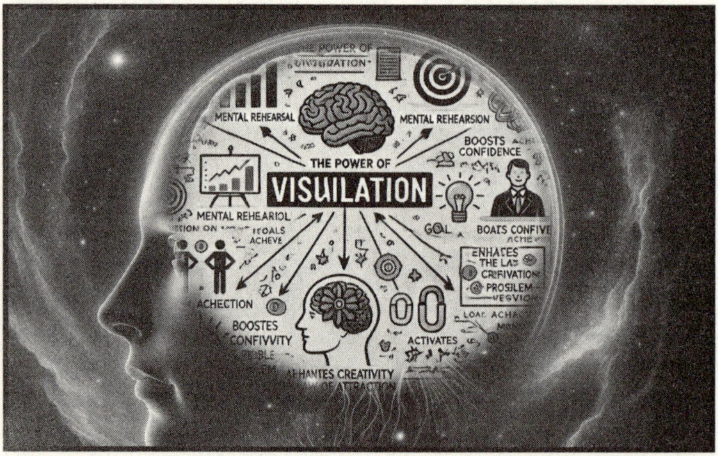

To visualize success is another aspect of the powers of the subconscious mind. It is critical to believe that you are successful in whatever you want to do or have started, rather than imagining so. Imagination is one side of the river while belief is the other. Therefore, it is important to understand the difference between these right at the beginning. The subconscious mind, an invisible presence in our body, is quite strange. It works on three aspects. The first is experience, the second is the goal, and the third is faith. Experience is at the centre. Faith and goal are far away from each other. However, as soon as someone starts to believe that he will accomplish a particular task, the subconscious mind starts devising ways to take this belief towards the goal, and a circle is completed. The person achieves success in his target. There is nothing in between to stop him, and he keeps advancing. That is why it is necessary to visualize that you are successful.

Visualize your dream life and financial success. See yourself achieving your goals. Visualization triggers the subconscious mind and motivates you to turn your goals into reality.

'The summit' is the only goal in the mind of a mountaineer. He is not scared of the many storms that may come on the way and all that can go wrong.

The specially abled New Zealand mountaineer Mark Inglis (both his legs were amputated below the knees) dreamed of climbing Mount Everest. He failed many times due to his physical condition or the adverse climate. But his subconscious mind kept repeating that he would succeed. Finally, in 2006, he climbed Mount Everest with his artificial legs. He became the first specially abled person to climb Mount Everest.

Japanese mountaineer Yuichiro Miura tried to climb Mount Everest for the first time when he was 70. He similarly had to endure failure many times due to poor health and age. But his subconscious repeatedly proclaimed his success. Ultimately, he climbed Mount Everest at the age of 80. He became the oldest person to climb Everest.

Arunima Sinha, a national volleyball player, lost one of her legs in an accident. Her subconscious mind pushed her to take up mountain climbing. She had to face multiple failures in it due to her disability. But the subconscious power of her mind was unshakeable. She did not give up and continued trying to climb again and again till she finally successfully climbed Mount Everest in 2013. She became the first specially abled woman mountaineer in the world to conquer Mount Everest.

There are many examples and stories of inspiring people who made the most impossible dreams materialize by facing challenges, purely with the power of their subconscious minds.

"Failures are but lessons that make us stronger for our goals."

No constraint or disability can be a barrier to this.

***

Chapter 32:

Setting Goals

When you are convinced that you are a successful person and you are going to achieve your goal easily, the first thing you should do is write down a roadmap for achieving the goal. Articulate your financial goals very clearly. Plan to walk through the big phases in smaller strides. It is necessary to pause occasionally if you want to travel very far. No player can win a marathon on the very first attempt. He starts to learn through experience by participating in smaller races of 100 meters, 200 meters, 400 meters, 800 meters, and 1500 meters, and then goes on to win a marathon of 42.195 km. If the goal is clear, then the subconscious mind advances in that direction, and the chances of success are manifold. But if the goal ahead is hazy, then even the power of the subconscious mind cannot do much, which is why it is necessary to determine checkpoints on the way while deciding the destination. The line will stretch to the destination when they are joined.

Setting goals is the most important step towards success in any task. It imparts clarity, direction, and motivation to complete any task. When you set goals and make a plan to achieve them, the chances of success are improved.

A few advantages will outline the importance of goal setting. Firstly, it provides a direction as to what to do and where to go. It helps you focus your time and energy in the right direction. It gives a boost to your motivation. It makes your goals clearer, and clear goals keep you motivated and give you the courage to move forward despite difficulties.

Secondly, it also provides a basis for measuring progress. If a goal is set, you can measure your progress and verify if you are proceeding in the right direction or not. An added benefit is that it boosts confidence. If you achieve one smaller goal, naturally, you feel more confident about reaching the next. This helps in further success.

***

Chapter 33:
The Importance of Goal Setting

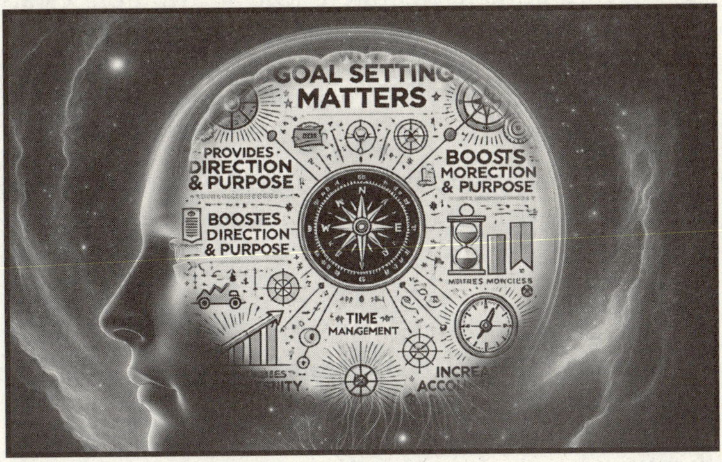

Goal setting provides a foundation for completing any task. It facilitates the way ahead for the subconscious mind. What does the subconscious have to search for if it has no idea what to achieve? Here, let's have a look at some of the advantages of goal setting:

1. **Focus**: It does not let your energy dissipate all over. The subconscious mind takes you in the right direction. It knows the entire route like Google Maps. From time to time, it also shows shorter routes and keeps giving suggestions.

The result of moving in the right direction is also visible.

2. **Positivity**: The feeling of moving closer to your goals each day will motivate you to reach your destination. Then you won't end up saying that the destination was just a step away from where you gave up.

3. **Promise of Success:** A clear-cut plan and commitment definitely lead to triumph. Goal-setting is considered to ensure success. Thinking about something does not assure success. How serious you are about your thoughts also matters.

When Henry Ford had the target of making the first engine, his goal was to manufacture "cheap, simple and sturdy cars which would be easily accessible to the common man too."

When Henry Ford, born in Greenfield Township in Michigan, U.S.A. in 1863, dreamt of making a vehicle that not just the rich but even people with average income would also buy, it was really challenging in those times.

His subconscious guided him, and he set a goal of mass production. With large-scale production, a vehicle that would be cheap enough and affordable to the common people could be made. In those days, cars were made only for the rich. Henry Ford's targets were laborers, farmers, and industrial workers. He started to work on his goal of 'mass production.' Ford used the assembly line method to manufacture his car. It was a revolutionary process, which reduced the cost of production and made car manufacturing faster. It was the result of his thinking that this became possible. Ford's engines and cars were so cheap that they became accessible to people of every class. His simple and durable engine not only simplified transportation but also brought about the Industrial Revolution.

Focus on the goal shortens the distance to achievement.

***

Chapter 34:

Hard Work and Smart Work

Whatever the task, the same old proven method known as SMART should be used for setting goals. The SMART method is quite useful for goal setting. The first letter 'S' in the acronym stands for Specific. It means that your goal should be clear and precise. For example, "I will lose 10 kg of weight in 6 months." If you wish to lose weight but don't set a goal, you may lose 1 kg and gain back 2 after some time; sometimes you may lose 3 kg, only to gain 5 kg later.

The second parameter of goal setting is 'M' – Measurable. The goal should be measurable so that the change can be clearly felt. It should not be left to guesswork. Let's say, if you think of losing some weight in the next week, there is no clarity about how much weight is to be lost. Chances of getting success in this case are therefore doubtful. But if you think, "I will lose 1 kg of weight every week," the chances of success will increase.

The third word is 'Achievable.' The goal should always be practical and achievable. You should not decide on something just because someone said something to that effect. Say, if you hear someone say that selling cow *ghee* is a very profitable business these days, and you start planning to buy a cow without having any money in your pocket, it's of no use. You don't have the necessary experience or the means to keep a cow; you don't even know how to make *ghee*, so how will you be successful? That's not possible at all. One more example is a goal that "I will exercise 30 minutes every day." This is feasible. But if you think that you would exercise 3 to 4 hours daily, how will it happen? You just don't have enough time to do so.

The fourth letter is 'R,' which implies that your goal should be 'Relevant' to what you want to do. You should not be going behind it because you have seen someone else do it or have heard about it from someone else. The subconscious mind will be able to accept the goal that you want to achieve only if it is relevant to your own life and ambitions. Otherwise, it will take a lot of time.

For example, consider the thought, 'weight loss is crucial for a healthy lifestyle.' It will be a goal easy to move towards. Because your subconscious also accepts that being healthy is better for your lifestyle.

The fifth letter is 'T.' T stands for 'Time-bound.' This is the most important requirement. You must clearly decide how much time you will take to do it to achieve the goal. You cannot simply leave it open-ended, hoping, "I will do it (someday)." You should say, "I will complete it in three months."

Every goal should have a definite timeline. Otherwise, the goal will keep moving away, and you will keep chasing it. For example, it is better to think, "I will reach my goal in 6 months," rather than just thinking, "I will achieve my goal."

If you adopt this SMART system of goal-setting, then no goal is impossible to achieve, whatever it may be. You clearly know what you have to do for it.

***

Chapter 35:

Dividing the Goal

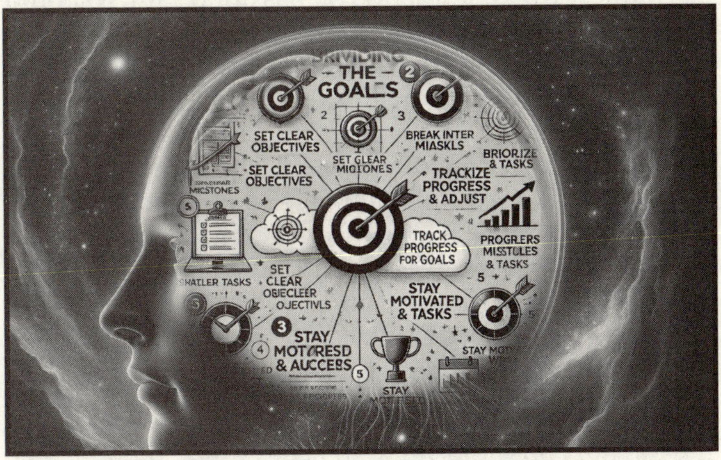

You can formulate strategies for achieving your larger goals. This will make reaching your targets easier. The first thing to do to get there is to write down your goal. You should write it on paper. It will thus always be in your sight. You can even paste it into a place where it will be in front of you. This proves to be very beneficial. Looking at it makes your brain more committed to those goals every moment.

Divide your larger goals into smaller ones. The advantage of doing so is that while achieving a small goal is easier, whenever you achieve a smaller goal, you will feel more energized and charged to move ahead wholeheartedly and zealously towards the next. You will enjoy satisfaction in achieving every small goal and remain highly motivated.

While you do this, you also need to prioritize your goals. Decide which goals are most important and which ones are to be achieved later, so that you can decide what to focus on first.

Making a detailed action plan is important. It should be exhaustive, covering all the finer aspects. Divide it into daily, weekly, and monthly tasks. While doing this, do not forget to ensure that the plan is practical and effective. It should not be distracting. The next rule is that it should be reviewed regularly. Reviewing your progress will keep you motivated and also keep you away from going off track from the goal. In case you are going astray from your path, the review will help you make the necessary improvements in your plan and bring you back on the path towards your goal.

Never get scared by obstacles. You may face them at any time, but you should have enough self-confidence in your subconscious mind to believe that 'there will be no obstacles.' A failure or hurdle should not leave you anxious. They will definitely go away.

"Success is enduring, failure is only temporary."

Learn your lessons from failures and continue your efforts. Lessons are indispensable to achieving any big goal. No one ever directly reached the pinnacle without climbing the steps.

***

Chapter 36:

The Importance of Affirmations

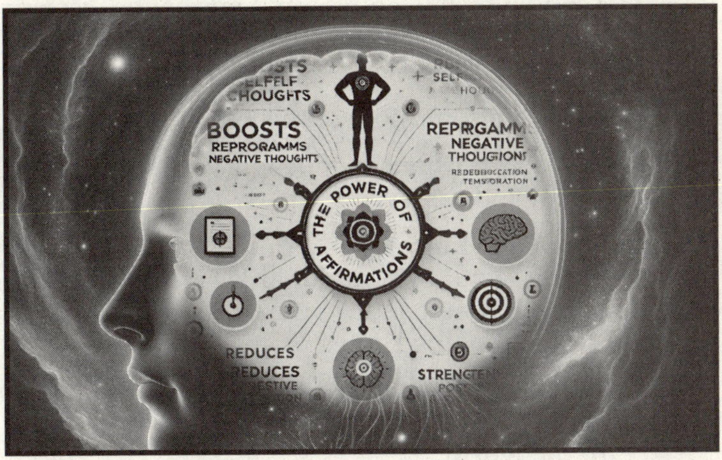

One should ensure that the subconscious mind always maintains a positive outlook. You should always believe wholeheartedly that you will achieve your goal. You have to do it with complete confidence. Motivational thoughts and affirmations can be very instrumental for this. Always read stories of people who have been successful and wealthy despite adverse circumstances. This will perk up your motivation and confidence and stimulate the subconscious mind. Participate in conversations only with people who have positive mindsets. A failed person will neither give you good counsel nor will he be pleased with your progress. They are not likely to say anything nice about what you have achieved. When two people argue, their egos are active in the background. Whenever you participate in conversations, always pause intermittently to assess whether you are being a victim of the same. Otherwise, the conversation is likely to get bitter. Many times, even the correct arguments may sound incorrect when our thinking is clouded by ego. Always try to avoid it. What's right or wrong can be analyzed later.

Your soul, which is nothing but your subconscious mind, will always tell you what's in your favor. You can even consider some good examples of this.

That is the very purpose of this book.

Here are some instances of people who started with a specific goal and achieved it:

1. **Abraham Lincoln:** He lost many elections, but his goal was **'national service.'** He never faltered from it and went on to become the 16th President of the United States.
2. **Thomas Edison:** He suffered 1,000 failures before inventing the bulb. His goal was to **'light up the world.'**
3. **Steve Jobs:** Giving **'excellent technology'** to the world was his goal. He made Apple the most valuable company in the world.

What I call the voice or power of the subconscious is nothing but the call of their subliminal mind.

Thinking of something great for the world is the shortest way to reach your goal.

***

Chapter 37:

The Power is Within You

We have so far discussed:

- What is the subconscious mind?
- What are the powers of the subconscious mind?
- What can be achieved through these powers?
- Has anyone used these before us?
- What needs to be done to achieve these powers?
- What are their benefits?
- Does it stand the test of science?
- What is the first step to obtaining these powers?

Now, we know what needs to be done to master the powers of the subconscious mind.

If one understands in entirety that the world's mightiest powers reside in our body and can be accessed to be successful, one can move closer to the secret of attaining them.

The ways of awakening the powers of the subconscious can be classified into two. The first is to master them yourself, and the second is to awaken them through another person.

The first way is to achieve it yourself. It is quite simple. It can be done through meditation and improving yourself.

Hindu scriptures very clearly explain the process of meditation. The whole world acknowledges it today. Regular meditation keeps the subconscious mind calm and focused. Replace negative thoughts with positive ones. Meditation helps one to fathom the cavernous depths of the subconscious mind.

Improving yourself implies improving your habits. For example, if you have negative thoughts, you should immediately discard them. One can never be successful in life with such thoughts, and this rule applies to every person. History is witness that no one with negative thoughts has ever been successful. Everyone successful has reached their destination only through imagination and positive thinking. When we have negative thoughts, they lead to psychosomatic disorders in our bodies. If this continues for long, we may develop stomach ulcers due to stress, headaches or migraines due to constant worry, or fatigue and physical pain due to depression.

***

Chapter 38:

The Magical Eleven

The human subconscious mind is infinitely powerful. Therefore, it has a deep impact on our habits, thoughts, and emotions. It can mentally, physically, and emotionally empower us if trained and awakened properly. Here are 11 effective techniques to awaken and use the powers of the subconscious mind:

1. **Develop Positive Thinking:** The subconscious mind soaks up both positive and negative thoughts. Repeat affirmations like "I am successful," and "my life is wonderful," every day. Of course, we have already discussed

this. We must always abstain from negative thinking and keep ourselves charged with positive energy at all times. Many people say, "I just can't give up alcohol." One such man approached me once. I asked him, "What's the difficulty? Why can't you stop drinking? Your wife is so unhappy about it." He replied, "I can't give up drinking because as the day turns to dusk, I feel that I won't be able to sleep if I don't have my usual peg." I explained to him that he was unable to give up liquor only because he had convinced his subconscious that he would be unable to sleep without it. It was he who was holding on to alcohol and not the other way round. "Why don't you challenge yourself to not drink liquor?" I asked him. He met me after a couple of months and told me that he had not consumed alcohol at all for a few months.

Work on developing positive thinking, not negative thinking.

2. **Auto-suggestion:** This is a very effective way of training the subconscious. Say your goals and desires aloud very clearly before going to sleep and after waking up. e.g., "I am capable of achieving my goals," "I am full of confidence," or "I can give up my negative habits." Continuous repetition of these leads the subconscious to believe that it is reality. It then starts creating ways for it to come true.

Swami Vivekananda wrote a letter to his disciple Mary Hale in 1896. He explains the powers of the mind and the subconscious mind in the letter:

"The subconscious mind is like a mighty reservoir. Whatever thought you impress upon it with conviction and repetition will shape your destiny."

3. **Meditation:** Meditation helps our subconscious to remain calm and clear. Meditate for 10-20 minutes every day. Focus on your breathing and keep your mind in the present moment. This will help develop the subconscious mind. We will later elaborate more about meditation.

4. **Use visualization:** The subconscious mind absorbs images and emotions more effectively. Visualize your desires and goals with complete clarity. Feel joy as if you have achieved your goal. Repeat this every day.

5. **Have faith in your subconscious:** The subconscious gets to work only when it senses your belief that something will happen. Have faith that your subconscious mind can solve every problem and fulfill your every goal. Cast away all doubt and make efforts with complete confidence. Do not allow negative thoughts like "I can't do this" to enter your mind. Maintain distance from those who discourage your ambitions. A positive environment strengthens the subconscious mind and promotes creative thinking.

6. **Set Clear Goals:** The subconscious mind quickly understands clear and concrete goals. I have also mentioned this earlier. Write down your goals and set out timelines. For example, "I will get a new job in 6 months." Repeat these goals again and again.

7. **Practice Gratitude:** Expressing gratitude fills the subconscious mind with positive energy. Express gratitude every day for all that you have. This habit helps in making your subconscious mind more positive. Expressing gratitude develops positive energy within.

8. **To be Happy:** Happiness is vital and effective. It brings mental peace and also improves physical, social, and professional life. Being happy is a positive attitude towards life. It helps us to face challenges, maintain health, and strengthen relationships. The benefits of being happy are also elaborated separately.

9. **Develop Good Habits:** Your habits directly affect your subconscious mind. Reflect on your habits and change them positively. Develop habits like getting up early, exercising regularly, keeping things in the right place, and completing every task on time.

10. **Control Your Words and Thoughts:** All our thoughts and actions have a deep impact on the subconscious. Therefore, one should be very careful while speaking. Never waste words on anything useless. Use positive words and thoughts while speaking. Repeatedly use phrases like "I can do it" and "yes, it is completely possible."

11. **Live in the present:** The subconscious mind is at its most effective in the present moment, as mentioned earlier. The subconscious never travels into the past or the future; it is always in the present. You also should avoid worrying about the past and the future. Focus on the present moment and engage in every activity

with complete awareness. It is important to note here that you are your subconscious mind. You are the only one who can keep negativity at bay and stay positive. The subconscious mind is no different from you. If your subconscious mind says that you will succeed, you will definitely succeed, because you are the one saying this.

Awakening the powers of the subconscious mind requires constant practice, a positive attitude, and faith. These 11 techniques can help you control and train your subconscious mind. When your subconscious mind works with you, you achieve success and satisfaction in every area of your life.

***

Chapter 39:

The Rewards of Being Happy

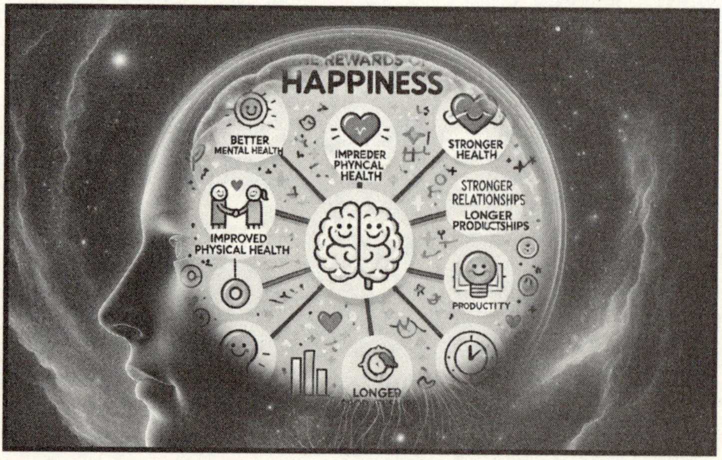

Happiness reduces stress. It releases stress and anxiety, reducing 'happiness hormones' like dopamine, serotonin, and oxytocin in the brain. Happy people are less likely to fall into depression and negative thoughts. Happiness broadens a person's thinking; therefore, happy people can find solutions to problems in a better manner.

It strengthens our body's immune system, resulting in a person becoming ill less often. A happy state of mind keeps blood pressure under control, thereby reducing the risk of heart disease. Research also shows that happy people, on average, live longer.

The Harvard Study of Adult Development found that there is a direct link between happiness and positive thinking. Another of its biggest advantages is that when the heart works well, i.e., if your blood pressure is under control and you speak unhurriedly, choosing the right words, listeners will listen to you very carefully and will not interrupt you.

The most important thing about being happy is that it improves relationships. Happy people choose good words. People tend to choose words that make others sad when angry. Happy people communicate better and build stronger social relationships.

Happy people naturally attract others and create a positive atmosphere. Happiness increases empathy and cooperation, leading to peace and harmony within groups and communities.

Happy employees and entrepreneurs are more motivated, creative, and productive. Positive thinking and happiness increase the chances of success.

Famous psychologist Shawn Achor explains in his book 'The Happiness Advantage' that happiness inspires success. This is, after all, about enhancing the powers of the subconscious mind.

Abraham Lincoln, the late President of the United States, said, "Most people are as happy as they make up their minds to be." If it is so, why should one set a limit to happiness? It should not be like, "I am happy as today there is a party or a wedding to be attended"; why? We can do this every moment.

Research of the Dutch Longitudinal Study found that happy people live 7 to 10 years longer on average.

Eleanor Roosevelt, the First Lady of America from 1933 to 1945, once said, "Don't let anyone else decide when and how to be happy. Happiness is in your own hands."

According to a Harvard study, happiness and long-term mental peace are directly related to physical health and good social relationships.

"Happiness is the elixir of life for the subconscious; it keeps the subconscious alive, don't let it be lifeless."

Expressing gratitude is a good start to being happy, as mentioned earlier. Express gratitude for little things.

Take care of your health, exercise regularly, and follow a balanced diet to be happy. Being happy promotes creativity. Devote time to your hobbies and interests.

Happiness gives a positive direction to every aspect of life. It is not just an emotional state, but a lifestyle. A person becomes mentally, physically, and socially better by adopting it. Feeling happy makes life more meaningful and satisfying. Therefore, it is necessary to adopt small actions and behaviors that make us happy and make them a part of daily life.

Do not forget to thank the Giver every day before going to sleep. Also, do not forget to offer all that you did throughout the day to Him. This will infuse you with new energy every moment of the next day. This is very easy to do and also quite effective.

Some people just are not capable of being happy. They keep telling their friends and family members about their problems all the time. Their subconscious mind believes itself to be caught up in a plethora of problems due to this. The veiled message here is that one should never believe that there are problems.

Happiness is achieved by being joyful; what is to really be attained is self-satisfaction.

***

Chapter 40:

Traditional Methods of Awakening the Power

The subconscious mind can be awakened through someone else. This can also be done in two ways. One is to do so under a *Guru's* guidance. This is really difficult in modern times. That's because who to have faith in is the personal call of each one. Not much can be said about this. A lot of people make lofty claims, but many also get duped.

Learning from a *Guru* was common in ancient times. Great *Gurus* and saints imparted knowledge about the subconscious and inner powers to their disciples. But it has now become difficult due to materialism and the lack of trust in the relationship between the *Guru* and the disciple.

A *Guru* is said to be the guide who takes one from the darkness of ignorance to the light of knowledge. A true *Guru* not only makes his disciple aware of inner powers but also inspires him towards the highest goals of life. Many great personalities, such as Chanakya and Chandragupta Maurya, *Swami* Vivekananda, and Ramakrishna Paramahamsa, belonged to the *Guru*-disciple tradition in the Indian culture. The *Guru* played a major role in enhancing the powers of the subconscious minds of the disciples in these relationships.

But today, it has become difficult to identify a genuine *Guru*. Many times, people masquerading as a *Guru* selfishly deceive others. In such a situation, it becomes the responsibility of each person to be cautious and direct their faith in the right direction. Understanding the teachings, behavior, and purpose is critical to identifying a real *Guru*.

People pay so much attention to the outside world in today's era that they tend to forget their inner world. Awakening the powers of the subconscious mind is not only helpful in achieving success and self-confidence but also essential for mental and emotional peace. Stress and competition have increased so much in modern life that people are becoming incapable of realizing their inner strength.

A person can bring positivity and balance in life by awakening the subconscious mind. This helps them face challenges and be self-reliant.

Awakening through a *Guru* and hypnosis are two distinct methods, with the same aim — to awaken the inner powers of a person. A *Guru* can only guide you towards the path; you have to walk on it yourself.

Whether you choose the path of a *Guru* or hypnosis, choosing carefully and with awareness is important. Identify a real *Guru*; get help from a trained and experienced person if choosing hypnosis. You must believe in yourself because ultimately, the power is within you. This is very important.

Awakening the powers of the subconscious mind and using them in the right direction is one of the biggest challenges and obligations in our lives. Both *Guru* and hypnosis are effective means to do so; but one should choose carefully between them, paying heed to the inner voice. Our inner power is the source of strength that can take us out of every difficulty and lead us to a successful, peaceful, and happy life.

***

Chapter 41:

Our Real Friend — The Subconscious Mind

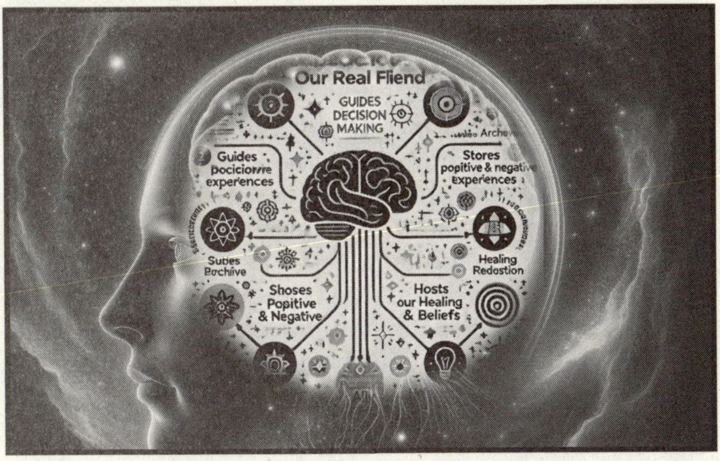

The connection between our body and the subconscious mind is not without any scientific reference. Science has tried to explain the connection between the body and the subconscious mind at many levels. This connection is elaborated in psychology, neuroscience, and mind-body medicine.

The subconscious mind influences every action of our autonomic nervous system. It has complete control over involuntary activities like breathing, heart rate, digestion, and blood pressure. Therefore, whenever we are anxious (even though we may not be fully aware of it), the subconscious mind activates the autonomic nervous system, which increases the levels of stress hormones (such as adrenaline and cortisol). This results in a faster heartbeat, increased blood pressure, and muscle tension. This is its way of keeping us away from problems caused by our anxiety.

The subconscious mind acts as a great healer for the body; if needed, it can even be a surgeon. We do not even realize when it restores disorders in the nerves. Many times when we get hurt, the doctor dresses up the wound, gives medicines, and asks us to come again after five to six days for a follow-up. During these five to six days, the doctor does not do anything; we take the medicines prescribed by the doctor. The wound starts getting better, but how does that happen? Who delivers the medicine to the injured nerves? It is the subconscious mind that understands the function of the medicine and carries it to the injured organ. But if you do not tell your mind that you have taken the medicine to get cured, the body will not be able to recuperate.

When a person believes that a drug or treatment will be beneficial to them, their subconscious mind triggers the body to respond through the placebo effect, even if the drug has no active ingredient. In scientific terms, the subconscious mind triggers the body to release endorphins (natural painkillers) and other positive neurochemicals, leading to tangible physical improvement.

It is our subconscious mind that is responsible for certain habits and automatic reactions of the body without our knowledge. Activities like riding a bicycle, swimming, or driving that we learn are recorded in the subconscious mind, and the body performs these automatically. When we are under stress, the subconscious mind switches the body into a 'fight-or-flight' response, even if there is no real danger.

It controls our emotions and related hormones. Every moment we feel happy, it releases happiness hormones like dopamine, serotonin, and oxytocin in the body. Similarly, when we feel scared or stressed, it increases the level of adrenaline and cortisol, so that there is no negative effect on the body.

In a state of fear and stress, it reduces the activity of the amygdala in the brain. Thereby, the heart rate slows down and stress reduces.

The subconscious mind can reorganize neuronal networks in the brain, resulting in a positive effect on physical and mental health. This phenomenon is called neuroplasticity. The subconscious mind can be trained to do this with the help of positive thinking and visualization.

***

Chapter 42:

Experimenting with the Subconscious under Hypnosis

Hypnosis is a mental technique that brings a person into a state of profound concentration and greater sensitivity to suggestions. It is also used to treat psychological and physical issues. Hypnotherapy is a recognized alternative system of medicine and is used to treat a variety of problems. The hypnotherapist is in complete control of the process, and though the subconscious is not in our hands, it is not far away either. Both these are two sides of the same coin. Anyone can be treated with hypnosis, as under hypnosis, the subconscious mind repeatedly tells the brain that the person has been cured. All these are the powers of none other than the subconscious mind, but the medium used is hypnosis. It is still used in many places across the world.

Hypnosis and the subconscious mind are deeply connected to each other because the main purpose of hypnosis is to reach the subconscious mind of a person and reprogram or direct it. Both can work deeply, affecting our thoughts, feelings, and habits. The purpose of hypnosis is to prepare the subconscious mind for positive changes. This process helps remove old habits (such as smoking, fear, or stress) and create new ones.

Information hidden in the subconscious mind, such as childhood trauma or negative beliefs, can be reactivated through hypnosis. It is used to transform these thoughts and bring about positive change. It sidelines the patient's 'critical faculty' and takes him into a deep meditative state. The conscious mind then becomes passive, and the person is free from external thoughts, obstacles, and negative perceptions. In this state, it is possible to directly influence the subconscious mind. It is hard to reach the subconscious mind under normal circumstances because our conscious mind is always active. Hypnosis bypasses the conscious mind by making it passive. This facilitates relaying suggestions and instructions directly to the subconscious mind.

This state is associated with alpha and theta waves of the brain when the brain is more receptive and calm. Our conscious mind normally prevents entry into the subconscious. But hypnosis slows down and inactivates the conscious mind, allowing direct access to the subconscious mind. In this state, negative beliefs like "I am a failure" can be changed to "I am successful and confident."

The subconscious mind creates your reality. It can be directed in the right direction through hypnosis.

***

Chapter 43:

Hypnosis as a Treatment

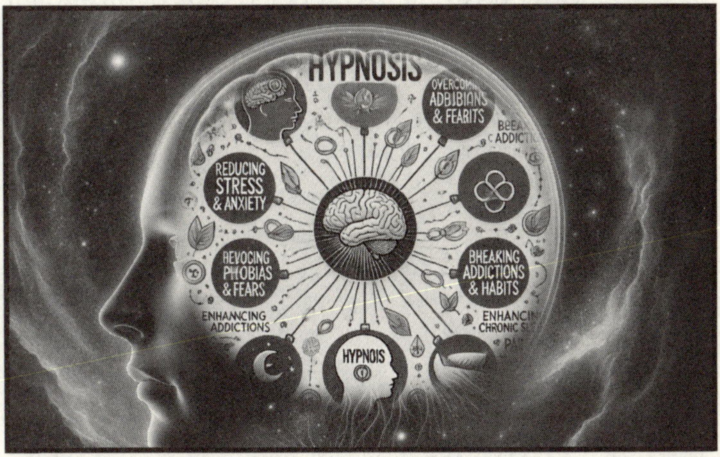

Any physical or even psychological ailment can be treated through hypnosis. It is in reality the subconscious mind that is active and resolves the problems during such treatment.

1. **Mental and emotional problems:** Hypnosis can be used to overcome psychological issues and improve psychological health:

   - **Stress and Anxiety:** Hypnosis calms the subconscious mind and helps to reduce stress. It is effective in boosting self-confidence and controlling anxiety triggers.

- **Depression:** Hypnosis can be used to change negative thoughts into positive ones. This ensures that the mind is completely tranquil.
- **Fears and phobias:** Many people suffer from fears of heights, water, society, etc. Hypnosis helps a person recognize their fears and overcome them.

2. **Correction of Bad Habits and Addiction Rehabilitation:** Hypnosis can help change harmful habits such as:

   - **Smoking Cessation:** Hypnosis reinforces the negativity of smoking in a person's subconscious mind so that they can give up the habit. For example, if someone wants to quit smoking, the positive suggestion "I do not need to smoke" given under hypnosis is quickly accepted by the subconscious mind.
   - **Overeating:** Hypnosis can change a person's attitude towards food for weight loss.
   - **Alcohol or drug addiction:** Hypnosis helps a person identify addiction and give it up.

3. **Treatment of physical problems:** Hypnosis can also be used to treat some physical issues:

   - **Pain Management**: Hypnosis can alleviate pain during the treatment of chronic diseases such as arthritis, migraines, or cancer. It trains a person's brain to change its response to pain. It is also possible to control pain during surgery. Hypnosis is used as an alternative to anesthesia in some cases.

- **Sleep Disorders**: Hypnosis helps a person go into deep sleep in treating insomnia or other sleep-related problems. It provides the option of drug-free treatment in many cases.

4. **Self-improvement and self-confidence:**

   - Hypnosis helps to develop positive thoughts and self-acceptance in the subconscious mind. This boosts the recipient's self-confidence.
   - Hypnosis helps a person to improve self-image and overcome the fear of speaking.

5. **Behavioural issues of children:** Hypnosis can be used to treat behavioral issues such as bedwetting, lack of focus, and fears in children.

***

Chapter 44:

The Modus Operandi of Hypnosis

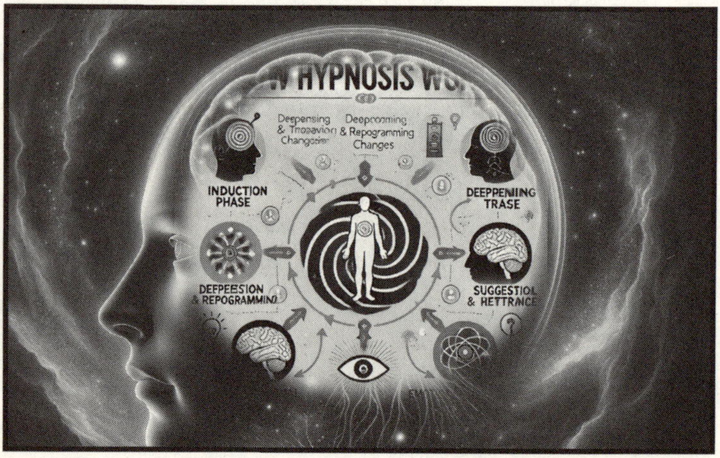

There may be an enquiry into how the subconscious works. Why does someone not accept something that is right or listen to their inner voice? The subconscious mind responds to emotions and suggestions rather than logic. If presented correctly, it is receptive to any idea without questioning. To comprehend this, we have to understand how hypnosis works.

State of deep concentration: A person is first taken into a calm and concentrated state of mind through hypnosis. This state unlocks the brain to absorb information at the subconscious level. The great Socrates believed that by asking questions to a person after deeply concentrating on him, the knowledge and truth hidden within him could be brought out. This process is a means of reaching the subconscious mind and unleashing its potential. He believed that a person can discover their intrinsic knowledge if asked the right questions.

For this, a person has to be taken to a state of deep peacefulness and meditation. Then it is done through breathing exercises, relaxing music, or slow instructions.

Once the person goes deep into the subconscious, they are led into deeper meditation so that the subconscious mind is fully activated. After this, positive suggestions related to their problem or goals are given. Finally, the person is slowly brought back to normal consciousness. The person then feels refreshed and calm.

***

Chapter 45:

The Don'ts of Hypnosis

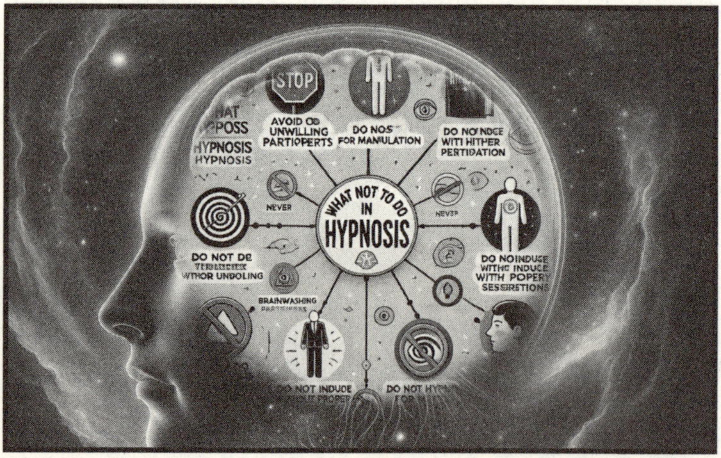

Hypnosis is an effective mental process, but it should not be used randomly in all situations. It is necessary to evaluate the mental, physical, and emotional condition of the likely recipient before using it. Using hypnosis can also prove to be harmful in some situations.

The therapist gives positive suggestions, like "you are being freed of negativity," or "you are brimming with confidence," or "you do not suffer from any disease," etc., during hypnosis. The subconscious accepts these suggestions and infuses them into the thought process and behavior of the recipient. After this, they are slowly brought back to a normal conscious state.

When Not to Use Hypnosis

- **Severe Mental Illness:** Hypnosis should not be used to treat conditions like schizophrenia, psychosis, or bipolar disorder. It can be harmful. Trying to influence the subconscious mind through hypnosis can worsen such conditions. The patient's mental confusion and fears may increase due to hypnosis.

- **Lack of experienced therapists:** Treatment should be administered only by a certified and experienced hypnotist. Hypnosis done in the right way is safe and effective. It can work quickly with appropriate sessions, and the chances of success are higher.

- **In a state of extreme fear or distrust:** If the recipient is extremely scared or distrustful about the process of hypnosis, it will not be effective. The person will not be able to completely enter the state of hypnosis due to distrust. This process can make the person more stressed or anxious.

- **In a very fragile mental state:** If a person is under extreme emotional stress, depressed, or suffering from suicidal tendencies, hypnosis is best avoided. Negative emotions hidden within the person may get aroused in such situations. This can worsen the situation instead of solving the problem.

- **Compulsion on children:** hypnosis can be used on children only when they are mentally ready for it, and the parents have consented to it. Forced hypnosis can have a negative impact on children's minds. They may often feel scared or confused.

- **Without medical advice for some medical conditions:** For an individual undergoing treatment for any physical or mental illness, hypnosis should be used only after consulting the doctor. Hypnosis should be avoided in case of serious physical ailments such as epilepsy or heart disease, as it can add to stress. Hypnosis should also not be used during pregnancy without consulting a doctor.

- **In case of extremely complex problems:** If the recipient's problem is deep-rooted and complex, e.g., addictions, severe phobias, or trauma related to sexual abuse, hypnosis should be used in combination with other therapies. Relying on hypnosis alone may not be enough. The help of a psychologist or psychiatrist is necessary in such cases.

- **Against the recipient's will:** Hypnosis can be successful only when the recipient accepts it voluntarily. An unwilling person should not be forced into hypnosis. Forced hypnosis can create fear and negative emotions in the person's mind. Hypnosis is a voluntary process, and it respects the psychological freedom of the person.

- **For entertainment or fun:** Hypnosis is a solemn process and should not be used for entertainment, fun, or to fool anyone. Doing so can harm the mental health of the concerned person. It also violates the basic purpose of hypnosis.

- **For violating ethical and legal boundaries:** Hypnosis should never be used to control or deceive someone or to commit a crime against someone. This is unethical and punishable under the law. Hypnosis should be used only for positive change and healing.

Use hypnosis only if both its purpose and process are positive and ethical.

***

Chapter 96:

Eternal Existence

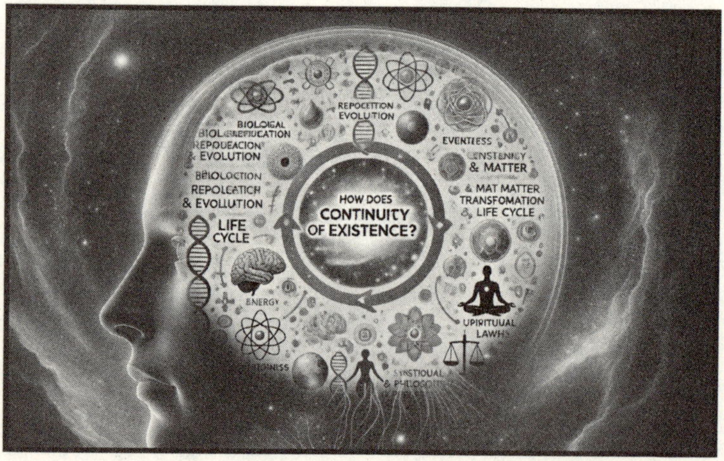

Fundamentally, you need a person you can trust, who can say that you are there, you exist, and you are great and worthy. Who do you think will say so? A man's thoughts are fickle and keep changing. If you say something agreeable to a person, he will feel you are nice. If you oppose another person's views, you become a bad person in his eyes. This has been the way people think of each other since time immemorial. Believe me, this is how it will always be. It's never going to change.

Humans understood this quite soon after the rise of humanity. That is how the faith in *Bhagwan*, God, *Ishvar, Allah, Baba* Guru Nanak, Jesus Christ, etc. originated. Man received strength from them, yet they would not say anything bad to him. They have only nice words to say. If it were not so, why would this conflict be there? If faith said that it is bad to hurt someone, to beat someone, then the believer would have given it up.

But it is not so. These conflicts will continue. People will not stop hurting others in the name of their faith. The subconscious needs some faith, which can give it strength. It is very necessary to have blind faith in someone to awaken their powers. For us, it can only be *Bhagwan*, God, *Ishvar, Allah, Baba* Guru Nanak, Jesus Christ, etc.

When we face a grave situation, **we pray to the power requesting it to save us.**

There's a person whose mother is in California. One day, he suddenly comes to know that she is unwell. Doctors say that anything can happen at any moment. His sister, who is with his mother, is doing what he is doing over here. Whether or not you go there to be with her, you would definitely pray to god to save your mother. The sister, who is near the mother, is doing the same.

Do you think the God who is with you here in Mumbai is also present in California with your sister? This is nothing but faith, and it works for sure. His mother is saved. The doctor's prognosis turns out to be wrong. Something like this has happened in everyone's lives at some point in time.

So, the first thing you must understand is that blind faith in someone is necessary to activate the subconscious.

My mother was on the verge of death. Doctors had given up hope and had told us to bring an ambulance to take her back home, as nothing more could be done. But my subconscious was firm that my mother had to witness the wedding of her only daughter before she left this world. I lied to her that my sister's wedding was fixed, that the wedding date was only a few days away, and that she had to get well.

Her health improved by the next morning. All the doctors were amazed. She was discharged from the hospital two days later in a much better condition. We had to admit her back into the hospital immediately after my sister's wedding was over and her *doli* was taken away. She left us forever after only a few days. It was the power of her subconscious that had kept her alive to see her daughter getting married. The power of the subconscious works so beautifully!

It is our *raison d'être*. It works covertly for us. All that is needed is that we have to keep motivating it to work favorably for us.

***

Chapter 47:

Treating Psychological Diseases

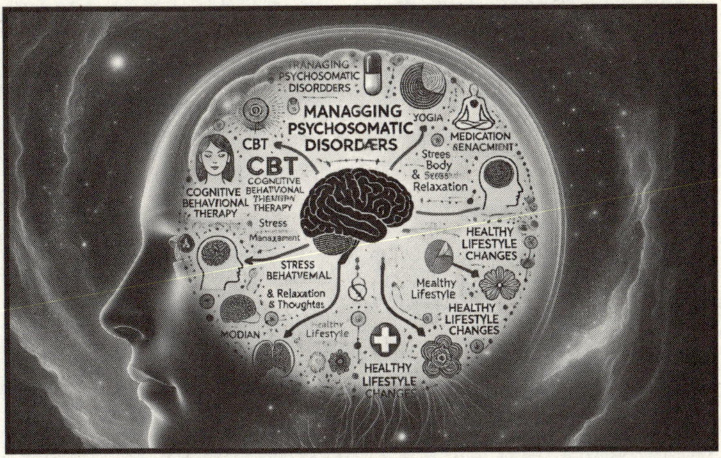

There are many registered examples of having treated diseases through psychology. It is called Psychological Therapy or Psychotherapy. The topmost among such therapies is Post-traumatic Stress Disorder (PTSD) treatment, also known as Cognitive Behavioral Therapy (CBT) or Exposure therapy. It is used to treat soldiers who have fought wars, victims of calamities, or people suffering from PTSD after disasters. This treatment can successfully restore the patients' normal lifestyle by curing the fear and anxiety related to PTSD.

The other is depression — a pervasive disorder, often treated through psychological therapy. It is known by the alternative names Cognitive Behavioral Therapy (CBT) or Mindfulness-based Therapy. A patient who was suffering from depression for a long period and was also a victim of suicidal tendencies was successful in changing his thinking and behavior with the help of a psychoanalyst. CBT administered along with medicines helped cure him.

People commonly suffer from phobias. Such patients suffer from some or the other phobia or fear. Phobia means fear. Its treatment is called desensitization or exposure therapy. A person suffered from aviofobia — the fear of flying. His psychotherapist was successful in treating his fear with this therapy. The patient's fear gradually reduced, and then he was able to travel by air.

A student who suffered from a phobia of public speaking was successful in enhancing his social skills with the help of psychoanalysis. The Social Anxiety Disorder therapy helped improve his self-confidence and helped him speak confidently in groups.

In case of complaints like stomach ache or migraine due to stress or anxiety, therapists treat the patient's psychosomatic disorders with such therapy.

All these therapies treat the subconscious mind of a person. They awaken its powers. That is how our existence continues and how we live. Happiness and misery, hope and despair, tears and smiles, are all expressions of our subconscious. They form the basis of our existence. We have to determine that we will only choose what gives us happiness. Only then our existence as a life will continue or we will get lost in hopeless despair.

***

Chapter 48:

Use of Hypnosis by the Famous

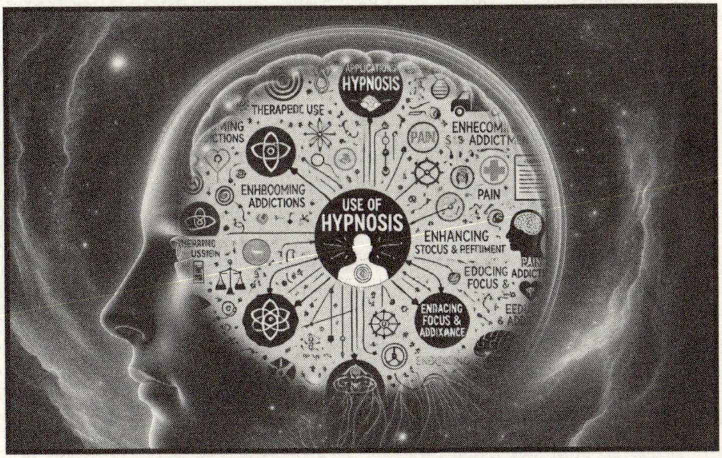

Many people, even famous personalities, have used hypnosis to get rid of their psychological and physical problems or habits. Here are some such people who have benefited from hypnosis:

1. **Winston Churchill**, the Prime Minister of Britain, was battling with extreme stress and insomnia during the Second World War. Churchill resorted to the use of hypnosis to sleep better at night. During the war, this helped

him retain his leadership capabilities and make crucial decisions.

2. **Tiger Woods**, the world's renowned golf player, used hypnosis to retain focus on his game and maintain confidence. He improved his mental concentration and stability, which resulted in taking his performance on the golf course to new heights. Woods accepted that he had used hypnosis to train his subconscious.

3. **Kevin Costner**, the famous actor and director, suffered from seasickness while shooting for a film in the high sea. He controlled it by using hypnosis and completed the shoot of his film *Waterworld*.

4. **Sir Edmund Hillary** used hypnosis to alleviate his psychological and physical pain during the climb of Mount Everest. Hypnosis enhanced his mental endurance and gave him the courage to climb the world's highest peak.

5. **Ellen Carr**, the British writer, was a chain smoker. His multiple attempts at giving up smoking had been unsuccessful. He gave up smoking with the help of hypnosis and also wrote the book *The Easy Way to Stop Smoking*, which helped millions to give up smoking.

6. **Mary Lou Retton**, the American gold medalist gymnast, resorted to hypnosis to retain psychological focus and improve her performance during the games. The enhanced self-confidence and mental grit helped her carve her name on the gold medal.

7. **Matthew McConaughey** is a famous actor who used hypnosis to bring about a change in his life

and to boost his confidence. It brought greater clarity to his life and career.

8. **Tom Silver** is a famous psychoanalyst. He has helped many people, famous and commoners, to overcome phobias and other psychological issues. He has helped thousands to change their lives through hypnotherapy.

The stories of these people are evidence of the effectiveness of hypnotherapy in reprogramming the subconscious mind and resolving psychological as well as physical problems. All of them were successful despite many obstacles by resorting to hypnotherapy as a tool, and they all benefited from it.

***

Chapter 49:

Use of Subconscious Powers by Criminals

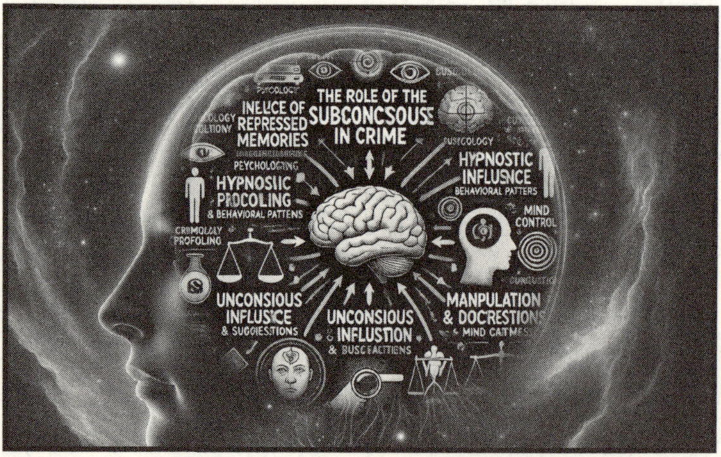

The Belgian Diamond heist involved the theft of diamonds, gold, and other valuables worth more than $100 million. The heist took place in Antwerp, Belgium, in 2003. The gang of thieves, called 'The School of Turin', breached the security of the Antwerp Diamond Centre. They broke into more than 100 safes. They disabled the centre's security system so efficiently that no one got a whiff of the theft until the next day. Some gang members were caught, but most of the stolen items were never found.

In March 1990, artworks worth $500 million, including paintings by Rembrandt, Vermeer, and other famous artists, were stolen from the Isabella Stewart Gardner Museum. This theft took place in Boston, USA. The thieves entered the museum disguised as police officers. They took the security personnel hostage and stole 13 priceless artworks. A bronze Chinese bowl and a Napoleon-era flag finial were also stolen. It is the biggest art theft ever. These artworks have not been found to date. A $10 million reward announced for information about the theft remains unclaimed to date. The theft took place on the night of St. Patrick's Day. Two thieves entered the museum donning police uniforms. They tricked the security personnel by saying that they had come to sort out a disturbance report. The security personnel were handcuffed and locked away in the basement. They roamed around the museum for about 81 minutes and stole 13 artworks. This confirms that this theft was very well planned. The museum's security system was weak. There were only two security guards, and the alarm system was outdated. The security guards were not trained and did not follow standards. Several suspects were questioned, but enough evidence was not found.

You will be surprised to know that the biggest thefts in the world were carried off using the power of the subconscious mind. The thieves chose people who had no lack of confidence. They must have mulled over each step and discussed it extensively while planning the robbery. They must have arrived at some decisions after that. Their subconscious minds must have answered their questions then. Come to think about it, who else would have answered it? That is why their plans were so formulated that even today, no one has been able to crack the thefts.

When we have an idea in mind and are convinced that this has to be done now, our subconscious starts planning for it systematically. It has only one goal then, that of fulfilling the thought successfully. Whether it is a worthy or a bad one depends on the intelligence of that particular person. Its only job is to achieve it successfully. It starts searching for ways to do so and frequently indicates to you how to do it.

Our subconscious mind has something that no human being can understand. All people with criminal tendencies carry in their subconscious mind the data of many crimes committed by them or others. It would answer their queries and doubts, and that is why they were successful. This example shows that one has to think very deeply to do anything successfully. One should never try to commit a crime.

If the police want to solve this case, they should bring together similar criminal masterminds and ask them to plan a similar operation. The suggestions they give during the planning process, and aspects they argue about, will give the police the clues they are looking for, and those criminals may also be caught. This is just a suggestion.

This example has been given only to show that there is no end to the powers of the subconscious mind; people have been using it for good as well as evil.

***

Chapter 50:

A Doctor under the Spell of Hypnosis

Franz Anton Mesmer (born 1734 in Egen, Austria) was a physician and the father of 'Mesmerism.' His contribution to the early development of hypnosis is considered to be very important. Mesmer developed a medical theory called 'Animal Magnetism,' which gained a lot of popularity in his time and later came to be called 'Mesmerism' after his own name. His theory of mesmerism is nothing but a combination of hypnosis and the subconscious mind. He used this as his medium. So, we can say that he was a doctor hypnotized by hypnosis. What he called magnetic energy was actually the powers of the subconscious mind, which worked even then.

Mesmer worked on the effect of magnetic energy on the human body. He believed that diseases were caused by the disruption of the flow of energy in the body and could be cured through 'animal magnetism.' He believed that everybody has an 'invisible magnetic force,' and its proper flow is essential to being healthy. Disruption in the flow would lead to a person becoming sick. He was talking about the subconscious mind, albeit unknowingly. Mesmer used magnets and his hands to restore the energy flowing in patients' bodies. He would take patients into a trance-like state, which is known as hypnosis or mesmerism today.

***

Chapter 51:

Philosophy and the Subconscious Mind

Besides Socrates, who was not the only person to ponder over the powers of the subconscious mind, there were many others whose philosophical thoughts about the subconscious, their ideology, and work have played an important role in the history of humanity.

The name of the Greek philosopher Socrates definitely deserves a special mention here. He is considered a great philosopher. If we understand his biggest idea, 'Know Thyself,' he actually discusses awakening and understanding the same latent powers of the human mind. He knew very well that the subconscious mind is mighty in itself. It has the power to cure any disorder. If we know ourselves, we will also understand our weaknesses, where we go wrong, and why we become sick. Then, through the powers of the subconscious mind, we can remain strong, accurate, and healthy.

The other formidable name is the great Greek philosopher Plato. He said that our soul is made up of three parts. The first is the intelligent and rational part. It makes decisions, rationalizes, and gives us awareness. He called it *Logos* (the rational mind).

He named the other part *Thumos* (will or emotional mind). This is the emotional and passionate element of the soul. It is connected to our courage, pride, and self-esteem. This is part of the mind we use most of the time.

He called the third part *Epithumia* (mind of desires). According to him, this is the primitive and subconscious part of the soul. It is responsible for desires for food, sex, and other physical desires. In fact, this third part completely corresponds to the concept of the subconscious mind. This is the part that drives our automatic and deep instincts.

We can apply the first part, *Logos* (rational mind), mentioned by Plato, to channel the powers of our subconscious mind in the right direction so that it makes appropriate decisions.

The second part of the soul, *Epithumia* (mind of desires), described by him, can also be inspired to make the right decisions by the powers of the subconscious. The allegory of the **'Myth of the Cave'** is perhaps his most famous idea. Here, he depicts human experience as a journey from ignorance to knowledge. He used to say that people living inside the cave only see shadows and consider them to be reality. They experience true light and reality when they come out of the cave.

Darkness in the cave may symbolize the subconscious, which controls our concealed instincts and thoughts. Coming out of the cave implies self-realization and bringing the powers of the subconscious mind into awareness. Thus, he too was far from or unaware of the powers of the subconscious.

To quote the great French philosopher René Descartes, "I think, therefore I am" ("*Cogito, ergo sum*"). If we reflect on it closely, this is the idea of our subconscious mind. If we do not believe in our existence, do we really exist? We may lose everything but our thoughts, and thoughts are purely a gift of our subconscious mind. If the power that is the source of thoughts is strong, then the strength will reflect in our thoughts as well. But if that power is weak, then, as Descartes said, "I do not exist." That is why we must strengthen the powers of our subconscious mind. Only then can the essence of our being be salvaged.

***

Chapter 52:

Swami Vivekenanda on the Powers of the Subconscious

The name of *Swami* Vivekananda of India is of great importance in discussions regarding the powers of the subconscious mind. *Swami ji's* thoughts about the importance and powers of the subconscious mind are profound. He believed the powers of the subconscious mind to be inexhaustible and that if trained properly, it could completely transform a person's life.

Swami ji had written in a letter to *Swami* Ramakrishnananda in 1895:

"He who always thinks of himself as weak and wild never becomes strong, but he who knows himself to be a lion, rushes out from the world's meshes, as a lion from its cage." (Translated from Bengali)

What he mentions here is nothing but the subconscious mind. It can be made into a lion through positive thoughts.

His basic outlook was that the subconscious mind remembers everything that happens in life. Therefore, the impressions on it are of great value. It is a storehouse of impressions of our past experiences (*sanskaras*) and actions (*karmas*). Every thought and action impacts the subconscious mind and shapes our habits and personality. If our thoughts are positive and pure, as an outcome, the subconscious will also be likewise. He also said that one can train one's subconscious through positive thoughts and self-suggestion. If you think that you are weak, your subconscious mind is going to make you so. If you think of yourself as someone strong, your subconscious will give you strength.

Swami Vivekananda said that 'confidence' is the 'power' of our subconscious. Confidence is a power in itself. When you believe in yourself, your subconscious mind turns it into reality. He repeatedly stated that success is impossible without self-confidence.

In this context, he recommended practicing meditation. *Swami ji* believed meditation to be the most effective way of controlling and purifying the subconscious. Through meditation, a person can become aware of deep thoughts and feelings hidden in their subconscious. Meditation makes one aware of the powers of our subconscious mind and helps direct them as per his wishes. He once wrote a letter to one of his disciples contemplating the subconscious mind:

"Understanding the levels of the mind is the first step towards purifying the soul. If we establish good thoughts and positive habits in our subconscious, it can bring miraculous changes in our lives."

He would also emphasize regular practice of self-realization as it facilitates understanding and controlling the subconscious mind and helps continued progress in life. He said, "When you are calm and your subconscious mind is balanced, you can experience your true nature (soul)." Vivekananda had so trained his subconscious mind that he could study and think deeply quite quickly.

Swami Vivekananda said, "We become what we think. If a person is always full of negativity, their life will also become the same. But if they are full of positivity, strength, and courage, their life will be wonderful."

***

Chapter 53:

Modern Society and the Subconscious Mind

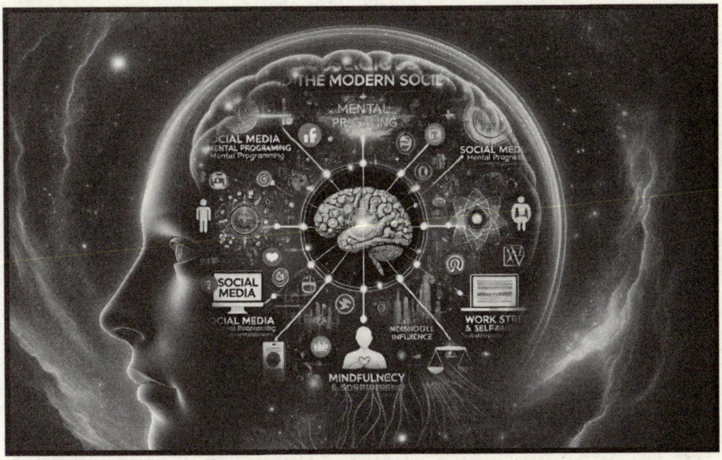

The holy men of India are constantly judged on the scale of truth due to some established dogmas. "How is it possible for someone to read someone's mind?" "How is it possible that they communicated with God?" "How is it possible that the fellow was cured of the disease by the mantra given by the *Yogi*?" "He is lying that he has a *siddhi*; *siddhis* don't exist," etc. But people who argue like this ignore the fact that the flock that has faith in *Yogis* and pious and holy men is ever-expanding. How is that happening? The answer is simple. They have faith in themselves, and the other person has faith in them. This bond of faith connects the subconscious minds of both. It is a reservoir of many such powers, and these *Yogis* and saints have obtained something from it with their penance, devotion, and dedication.

Lord Gautama Buddha, too, believed that "the mind is everything. You become what you think." This statement is a direct attempt to explain the influence of the subconscious mind. His theory of meditation and *Vipassana* preaches that one can understand one's *samskaras* and eliminate them completely. One attains peace and wisdom when the mind is freed from negative *sanskaras*.

Though you cannot see it, you believe that someone has travelled to the Moon or Mars, both millions of miles away. You think it to be true. Why do people keep pointing fingers at something proven right millions of times, then? This is a matter of faith, which is the essence of every religion.

Lord Krishna's *Geeta* is central to the Hindu religion. In *Geeta,* he says that man thinks he is the doer, but he is unaware that it is I who does everything. People try to deny this. When the American writer, satirist, speaker, and humorist Mark Twain, whose real name was Samuel Langhorne Clemens, said that "I have not done anything in my life, whatever I have done was done by my subconscious mind," people laughed. They did not see the veiled teaching of Lord Krishna in his statement that man, in reality, does not do anything; it is his subconscious mind, which is God or *Ishwar,* that gets everything done. That is why we must develop it in such a way that it acts only in a good way.

Lord Buddha said that the desires and attachments hidden in our subconscious mind are the root of our suffering. These desires and attachments are rooted deep in the subconscious mind. A person can eliminate these desires of the subconscious mind through meditation and the right (*samyak*) understanding.

When someone drives a car or a vehicle, they may simultaneously speak, think, feel sad about something, or sometimes get lost in happiness. All those who drive vehicles have experienced this very well.

Who does all this? It is our subconscious mind that remembers how the vehicle works, which road leads where, where the turn is, where the red light is, and if an animal suddenly crosses the road, we must use the brakes. It does all these tasks. It is very powerful.

But when did you or anyone else prepare it for all this? Unusual though it may sound, it is both the trainer and the learner. If it can remember the rules of driving, imagine how beneficial it can be in many fields.

***

Chapter 54:

Helping Others Silently

Sometimes people come to us and say, "Your friend or your brother behaved very badly with me, he has not returned my money yet," or they say, "I only think well of him," etc.

It may be that you also do not have a good opinion about the person in question, or he has behaved badly with you too. But remember that this is the acid test of the powers of your subconscious mind. If you also say that he is not good, or if you start talking about your past experiences, your subconscious mind will never forget this talk. As a result, whenever you are around that brother or friend, you are bound to say something unpleasant. You may have to face all sorts of problems in the future due to this.

Remember that time is never bound by anyone's wishes. Secondly, such things about someone also promote negativity in your mind. Speaking ill of others is evil, no matter why it is done. Even if you badmouth someone, thinking it to be true, it's bad. In the future, this will harm you and not the person who has done something bad. This is the ultimate truth. Accept this not because the scriptures say so, but because it will deplete the power of your subconscious mind.

At home, when your child or wife says sorry for the biggest of follies, you let go of everything on hearing it and assume that they will not do so again. You should remember this for everyone with a genuine intent. You should not discriminate while doing so; otherwise, your subconscious mind will be confused and will make wrong decisions. It does not know who your child is or who your friend is. It only appreciates the importance of the words you utter. The affection you show means everything to it.

Once, I went to attend a condolence meeting. The priest was giving his sermon, as we all sat facing him. Two gentlemen sitting in the back rows were lost in their own world, jabbering away. The priest said that the deceased, Umesh Babu, was such a good person that he never thought twice to help anyone. One of the gentlemen sitting behind was heard whispering, "I requested him once to allow me some time, I promised to repay his money two months later, but he did not agree and told my father everything. My father then returned the money to him. I am here today only on my father's insistence."

I thought, "Even in this place, on such an occasion, people do not listen to their minds. Has the goodness of their subconscious mind stopped communicating with them? What will anyone get except negativity by speaking ill of the dead?"

***

Chapter 55:

Simple Guidelines to Follow in Life

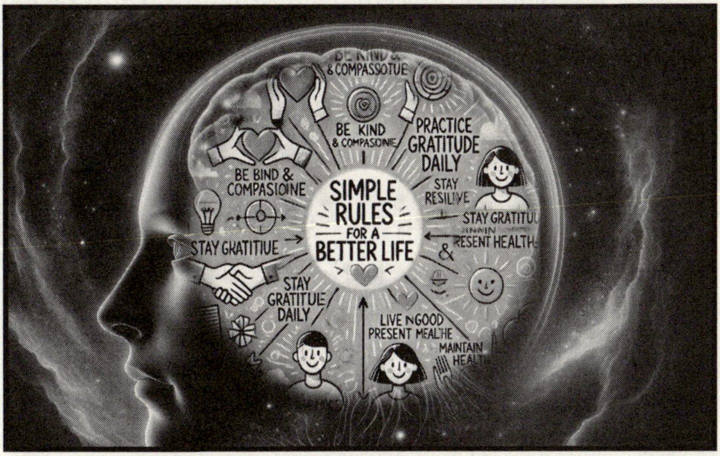

1. Plant a sapling with your own hands somewhere, whenever you can. You will never forget the experience, and when you see it grow into a tree, you will enjoy a unique feeling.

2. Help a stranger, but remain a stranger to them. Your mind will especially remember this.

3. Say thank you often. Expressing gratitude increases the energy of the subconscious mind.

4. Apologize to someone for something in person, in writing, or through a message.

5. Look in the eyes of a stranger on the road with a smile, as if they were your own.
6. When you look at a burning lamp, think that you have burnt all your negativity.
7. Don't suddenly jump into an ongoing conversation. Understand what it is about before joining it.
8. Remember that criticizing others diminishes your inner powers.
9. It is better to remain silent than to try to prove yourself. Keep in mind that someone who did not accept your truth the first time is not likely to do so in the future.
10. Opportunities do not knock again and again. One should be able to recognize them. This is possible only when you have such powers.

***

Chapter 56:

How to Meditate

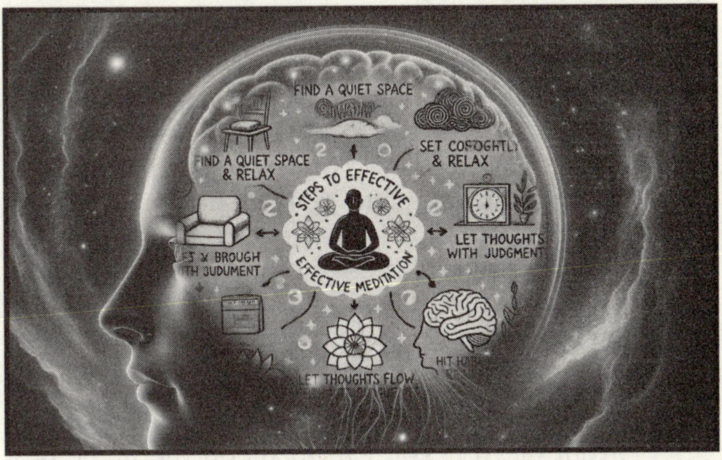

Meditation is a science our sages and yogis have known for a long time. There are five eternal truths that will not perish as long as mankind exists. These elements are called *Panchbhoot tatva;* they are the five fundamental elements – earth, water, fire, air, and sky. If you observe, the earth is transformed into water, water into air, and air into the sky. The sky is our mind or the subconscious mind. Therefore, the mind merges into the soul while meditating, and can hear the voice of the soul. The soul speaks nothing but the truth. That is why the feelings, answers, and decisions made while meditating prove correct.

All you have to do while meditating is merely to rise above the earth and water, transform into air, and raise the sky, i.e., your mind, higher and higher so that it can unite with the soul. Then you will see only the truth. Do not read this like a philosopher, but consider it to be science; only then will you be able to live a happy and trouble-free life by attaining the untouched, invisible powers of your subconscious mind and your body.

There are various methods of meditation that are used for different purposes and various mental, physical, and spiritual benefits. It has only one form, really, which is to focus the powers of your conscious mind on your subconscious mind. The aim of all the techniques of meditation is to awaken the powers of the subconscious mind. All these methods enhance mental peace, self-realization, and the ability to concentrate. The main methods of meditation are as follows:

1. ***Trataka* Meditation**: In this method, you have to keep staring at a point on a wall or paper in front of you. You can focus on the flame of a lamp or any shining object without blinking. This improves concentration and also calms the mind. You have to completely give up all your connections with the outside world while meditating.

2. ***Mantra* Meditation:** One has to sit comfortably on a mat and meditate while chanting any holy mantra such as *'Aum,' 'Aum Namah Shivaya,'* or *'Gayatri Mantra.'* This gives peace to the mind and awakens the soul, reduces stress, increases energy in the body, and one starts getting spiritual experiences. Even in the deepest sleep,

one does not feel as much peace as one does during this meditation.

3. **Breath Meditation**: In this method, you have to focus on your breath. It teaches you to live only in the present, and the mind remains calm. This reduces stress and increases self-awareness. You have to take a deep breath in, exhale, and focus only on the process of breathing. You will hear some sounds initially; they are just like sounds heard while pouring water into an empty vessel. As soon as it is completely filled, there will be no sound.

I was a young man when I had the good fortune of visiting Kashmir. I call it my good fortune because what I learnt there is still useful.

When my friend and I went to Kashmir, we travelled to Pahalgam from Srinagar for two days. We were planning to go to Amarnath from there. We did not know that one can visit Amarnath only during some designated months. We came to know about it only after we got off the bus in Pahalgam. There was a lot of time before the bus to go back. We had nothing to do but wait. We had some food in a restaurant there. Then, we noticed a river flowing nearby. We leisurely strolled towards the riverbank. As we walked, we realized that though the river had appeared to be close, it was actually quite far away.

We reached there and sat on a rock, enjoying the gurgling of the river.

A native Kashmiri man, probably grazing his cattle there, came near us after a while. My friend and I were talking to each other rather loudly. He suddenly said, *"Yaar, thod' won chup thavith paharan hyet soon."*

I asked him what it meant. He explained, "O' Friend! Be quiet for some time and listen to the mountains; they will teach you patience. Patience is the key; everything will be alright with it."

We did not utter a word after that and sat as still as those hills for a long time. In all honesty, the experience of that peace is still treasured in my subconscious mind.

1. ***Saguna* Meditation** (Meditation of a physical form): One concentrates on the physical form of a God, Goddess, or *Guru* in this method. One should envision their qualities. The purpose here is to establish a relationship with God or one's favorite deity. Our devotion increases, and we get spiritual peace as a benefit of this meditation.

2. ***Nirguna* Meditation** (meditation of the formless): In this process, one has to sit in a quiet place and concentrate on the formless *Brahman*, pure consciousness, or void. This is one of the more difficult methods. Yet, one can definitely be successful. Its purpose is to realize the reality of the soul and to create a sense of unity with the *Brahman*. One experiences deep spiritual peace and liberation with this meditation, too.

3. ***Vipassana* Meditation**: For this, one has to be aware of one's body, mind, and emotions. Its purpose is self-introspection and purification of the soul. This helps to maintain inner peace, self-control, and mental balance. During this meditation, one has to observe the experiences and thoughts arising in one's body and mind without reacting to them.

4. ***Chakra* Meditation**: For this, one has to focus on the seven energy *chakras* (from *Muladhara* to

Sahastrara) in the body. Through this meditation, the energy of the body remains balanced, and spiritual awakening occurs. It improves the flow of energy in the body and improves physical and mental health. For this meditation, one has to visualize the colors and energy of the *chakras* in the body and feel the energy flowing through them. This is the highest form of meditation. It takes a lot of time to master it.

5. ***Pranayama* Meditation**: In this method, one goes into meditation by controlling the breath. Its purpose is to increase the flow of physical energy and control the mind. As a benefit, mental stress is reduced, and the balance of energy is maintained. Begin with a deep breath to do this meditation, hold it for some time, and exhale slowly. Repeat this again and again.

6. **Transcendental Meditation (TM)**: One enters into a deep meditative state, chanting a special *mantra* received from a *Guru*. This method should be practiced only after learning it from a qualified teacher or *Guru*. The inner peace of the mind is maintained, and the body begins to go into a state of deep relaxation. Practicing it brings about obvious enhancement in mental clarity and reduces stress.

7. **Nature Meditation**: For this meditation, one has to concentrate on the elements of nature, such as trees, water, sky, or the sound of birds, with full faith. When our subconscious mind starts feeling connected with nature, we experience inner peace. This eliminates all types of stress from the body. When yogis practice this meditation, the duality between the object they are meditating on and their mind vanishes.

> The object becomes subject to the power of their subconscious mind. At that time, if they want, they can then even make the physical object levitate. Ancient Indian texts have many references to *yogis* and *siddha purushas* who could move objects with their meditation and mental concentration.

I once got a chance to visit Switzerland with my family. We visited many places there. True to its fame, each one was more beautiful than the previous. We reached Zurich, traveling around. Once, I was roaming alone in the market there in the evening. It started raining lightly. So I stood under the awning outside a shop on one side. Another man who looked like he was from India was also standing there. I started talking to him. He told me that he lived there now. He hailed from Kerala. He had come there eight years ago and had been there since then.

I casually asked him whether he had decided to live in Switzerland because it was such a beautiful country.

Then he narrated an old fable to me, "Eight years ago, when I came here to stay for a few days, someone told me a story. When I heard it, I felt I must spend the rest of my life here." He continued, "The mountain peak you see there in the front is named 'Emil Hill'. It is named after a shepherd. Long ago, this was a small village situated amidst the beautiful and peaceful valleys of Switzerland. An old shepherd named Emil lived there. Emil used to spend his day grazing his sheep in the lush green valleys. All around him were tall mountains covered with snow, which seemed to touch the sky. He was just an ordinary shepherd for the villagers. Emil really was a man with years of deep spiritual experiences and possessed a deep spiritual understanding. They came to know this only later."

The story continued. Emil would climb up a soaring hill every morning where the peaks of the Alps touched the sky. He would sit there quietly, closing his eyes, listening to the blowing wind whisper.

When he would come back, villagers would often ask him, "Emil, what do you hear?"

Emil would smile and say, "The hills speak to those who listen not with their ears but with their souls. Going there fills my subconscious with joy." The man said, "And I've been here ever since."

When I heard the story, I wondered if I, too, could listen to what the beautiful mountains and cold breeze whispered to him.

I sat on a roadside bench for a long time after it stopped raining and listened to a myriad of sounds. Nature really replies when we crave to talk to it. You should try it too.

Serene natural beauty sometimes gives us a profound message of self-exploration.

***

Chapter 57:

Miraculous Powers of the Subconscious Mind

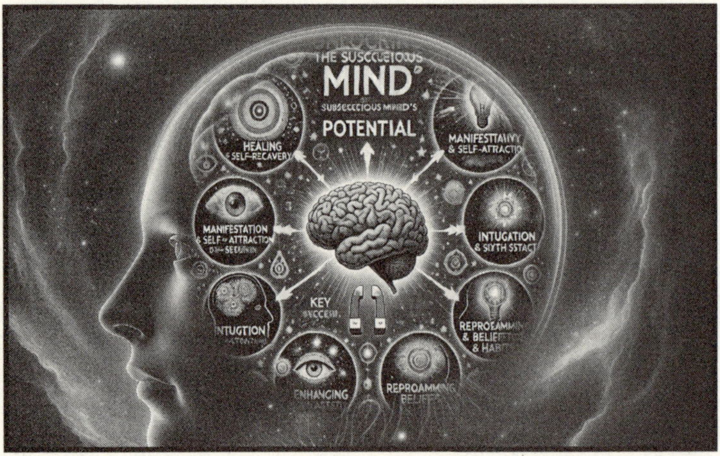

Telekinesis is a type of psychological power. **Uri Geller** is famous for his mental powers. He claimed he could bend spoons with his mental focus and move objects with mental energy. His performances were challenged in scientific experiments and were often seen as magic tricks. He was born on 20 December 1946 in Tel Aviv, Israel. He became very popular in Europe and America in the 1970s and 80s.

Uri Geller participated in some experiments at the Stanford Research Institute (SRI). These tests claimed to confirm his psychic powers. He is 77 years old now. He also has a website named urigellermuseum.com.

Three more powers of meditation can be added to his power:

1. **Silent Meditation**: It involves remaining in complete silence in a quiet place to experience the energy and peace within oneself. Through this meditation, we are able to reflect on ourselves in our bodies. Practicing this gives a feeling of deep purification of the soul.

2. **Dynamic Meditation:** Here, people meditate through physical activities such as dance or movement. It should be done without any interruption. This removes the obstacles between the body and mind. Our physical and mental energy gets a boost then.

3. **Meditation with Yoga**: This is done with *yoga asanas* and reflection. Its purpose is also to maintain the balance of body, mind, and soul. This maintains our physical fitness, and we begin to experience mental consciousness. One should be able to go into deep meditation after practicing *yoga asanas* for this process.

***

Chapter 58:

Selecting the Right Method of Meditation

A lot of caution must be exercised while choosing the method of meditation. The suitable method of meditation varies depending on the needs and experience of each person. Meditation needs to be practiced regularly for it to be beneficial. Only simple methods should be chosen in the beginning.

***

Chapter 59:

An Experiment with Self

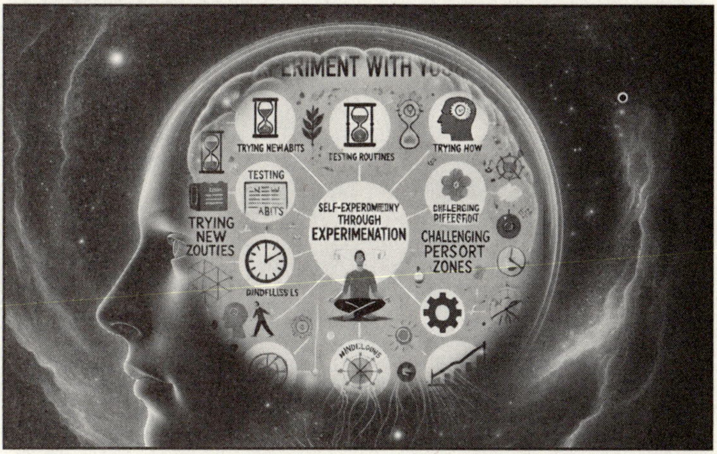

You have understood all that I have written so far, and now you also want to achieve it. If you have reached this far, I am absolutely sure that one day you will also achieve all of it. You should conduct an experiment on yourself at home after a while; when you have spent a good length of time in meditation, your mind has also become calm, and people have started telling you that you have become very composed, your anger has also vanished, or you have gained complete control over your anger.

Take a large glass or bamboo pot, about two inches deep, and place it on a table in front of you. Keep it at a distance of 3 to 4 feet. What you have to do is sit blindfolded on a chair in front of the pot, with a couple of tennis balls. Throw the balls forward, imagining that all the balls are falling inside the pot.

Keep practicing this regularly with the conviction that in a few days, the number of balls falling inside the pot will increase. The powers of your subconscious mind will keep growing with this practice, and they will be useful to you in life.

***

Chapter 60:

Some Perplexing Queries

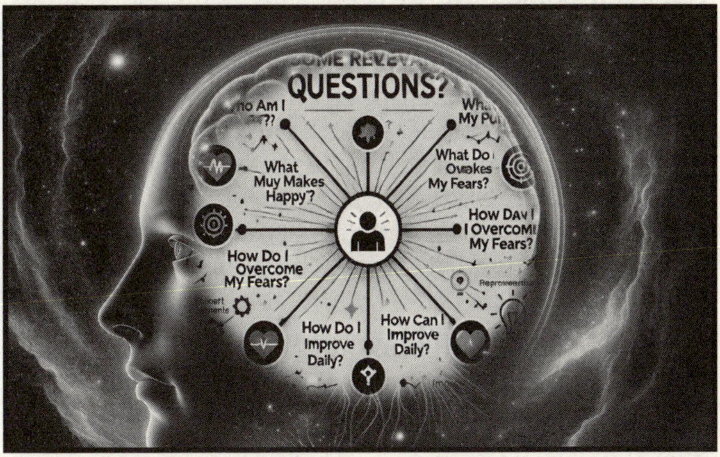

If the subconscious mind lives only in the present, how will someone's subconscious mind accept for the first time that such powers exist? The particular person may not have any relevant previous experience.

The subconscious mind of that person may not accept that this can happen immediately when the person comes across it for the first time. That is why it is being said right from the beginning that it will have to be continually repeated that "this is possible." By doing so, it accepts that this is possible. You have to keep in mind that it lives only in the present. You are repeatedly telling it that this is possible only in the present. Our minds definitely have such powers.

If a person tells us something based on their past experience or we read about someone's experience in a book, our subconscious mind does not believe it, as it does not have that experience.

The first thing one should understand is that when you read something in a book or someone explains something based on their experience, then anyone's subconscious mind, called *Epithumia* (mind of desires), accepts it; it does not reason about it, but simply accepts it. It is our conscious mind, which is called *Logos* (rational mind), that reasons and rejects it. It has been mentioned over and over again in this book that our subconscious mind accepts everything without giving any reasoning, and it quickly accepts if something is said repeatedly.

Is intense meditation necessary to awaken the dormant consciousness of the subconscious mind?

No, it is not like that at all. Meditation helps the dormant mind to believe quickly, that's all. If someone accepts the positivity of something or a goal and repeats affirmations like "I will definitely achieve it," or "It is not difficult for me to achieve it," then the goal can be achieved even without meditation. Meditation only makes the path easier.

Does the subconscious mind carry our awakened powers to the next life after death?

There is nothing in our body that can take anything happening in this life forward to the next life. Besides, as the subconscious mind lives only in the present, there is no question of it taking anything forward. It does not go into the future; it lives only in the present.

However, some gods and demigods are exceptions. Ravan was a courtier named Vijay in Lord Vishnu's court in his previous birth, as mentioned in the *Kartik Mas Mahatmya* of *Skanda Purana*. He became Ravan in his second birth, and his third birth was as Shishupal in the *Dwapar Yuga*, when he was killed by Shri Krishna. We see here that in all three births, he had all the powers right from birth. So were these powers already present in his subconscious mind? This is the question.

***

About the Author

Rajesh Takyar was born in Punjab and brought up in Jalandhar and Delhi. He graduated with a B.Com (Pass) from Delhi University. His first book, *Inventing Dreams*, won the Golden Book Award 2025. His second novel, *Diary of a Monk*, was well received by the people. His third book, *Krishna Ek Satyagyan*, and fourth book, *Safalta Ka Rahasya*, have changed people's lives.

He currently lives in Haryana. His new novel *Sinop Ka Khazana* became a topic of discussion even before its release, and is now being called the best mystery novel. He is also on the path to publish a 18-book series titled *Shrimad Bhagwad Gita*.